O9-AHW-509

THE TIGER INSIDE

THE TIGER INSIDE

A New Approach to Caring for your Cat

David Alderton

HOWELL BOOK HOUSE
NEW YORK

A Quarto Book

First published by Howell Book House
A Simon & Schuster Macmillan Company
1633 Broadway
New York, NY 10019

MACMILLAN is a registered trademark of Macmillan, Inc.

Library of Congress Cataloging-in-Publication Data
A catalog record for this book is available from the Library of Congress

ISBN 0-87605-611-7

This book was designed and produced by
Quarto Publishing plc
The Old Brewery
6 Blundell Street
LONDON, N7 9BH

Senior Editor Gerrie Purcell
Copy editor Eleanor Van Zandt
Art Editor/Designer Julie Francis
Photographers Bruce Tanner, Les Wies
Illustrators Robert Morton, Janice Nicolson
Picture Research Zoë Holtermann
Editorial Director Pippa Rubinstein
Art Director Moira Clinch

Manufactured by Universal Graphics Pte Ltd, Singapore
Printed by Star Standard Industries (Pte) Ltd, Singapore

CONTENTS

CATS: FROM

THE WILD

Just how like their wild relatives are today's domestic cats? The answer is that they are remarkably similar, in spite of the divergence caused by domestication, which began over 9,000 years ago. Many of the behavioral traits seen in wild species can still be observed in domestic cats. As a group, the cat family has proved highly successful, and domestication has taken cats to many isolated islands around the world where previously none existed.

Sadly, in some cases, this has caused great environmental harm, especially where there have previously been no major predators. The cats introduced by settlers have posed a serious threat to ground-nesting and flightless birds in particular.

The domestic cat retains the anatomical features and senses of its wild relatives, with the result that if abandoned, it is likely to be able to revert to a free-living existence. Such cat populations are described as feral.

CAT COUSINS

Today's domestic cat still bears a striking resemblance to the other members of the cat family. Wild cats have evolved on all continents except Australia and Antarctica, and amazingly, during the 1980s, another large, previously unrecognized species was found to exist, bringing the total number of wild species currently known to 38. There could still be others yet to be discovered.

Small cats of the old world

Wildcat
(Felis silvestris)
Europe, Asia, and Africa
Two distinct populations — in Eurasia and Africa. The latter is thought to be the ancestor of today's domestic cat, being much more friendly than its European counterpart. It also has a longer, tapering tail — a feature associated with domestic cats, but not with the European wildcat.

African golden cat
(Felis aurata)
Africa
In spite of their name, these cats vary considerably in color, with some being much grayer than others. Spotting of the coat is also apparent in some cases. African golden cats have a reputation for being very aggressive if cornered, and they are able to hunt off the ground, if necessary.

Jungle cat *(Felis chaus)*
Middle East to Asia
Found in a variety of habitats, ranging from reed beds to rain forest. Able to climb and swim well. Feeds on a variety of prey, from frogs to deer fawns, and has been known to eat olives.

Temminck's golden cat
(Felis temmincki)
Asia
Closely related to the African golden cat, although these two species are now separated by a distance of around 4,300 miles (7,000km). Has a slightly heavier build and equally variable coloration. The young can become tame and affectionate toward people.

Pallas's cat *(Felis manul)*
Asia
This cat's long coat helps to provide protection against the cold. It retreats into burrows during the day. Said by some to have contributed to the development of the Persian longhair domestic breed, but this view is not widely accepted today.

Iriomote cat
(Felis iriomotensis)
Asia
Another species with a very limited distribution — confined to the island of Iriomote, south of Japan. Became known to science only in 1967. Males will fight fiercely with each other over a female prior to mating. The total world population of these wild cats is estimated to be just 100.

Chinese desert cat
(Felis bieti)
Asia
A species that lives in steppe land rather than desert. Thought to hunt mainly by hearing, but very little is known about these particular wild cats and their life style.

Leopard cat *(Felis bengalensis)*
Asia
Large numbers have been killed for their fur in recent years. Patterning and color vary through their range, which extends to the Philippines. Usually have only two or three kittens in a litter. Have recently been hybridized with domestic stock to produce the Bengal breed.

Bornean red cat *(Felis badia)*
Asia
Confined to the island of Borneo, off the southeast coast of Asia. Very little is known about this species, which is also known as the Bornean red cat, because some are of this color. Another form is grayish. Reputed to catch monkeys in trees. Has only small upper premolar teeth.

Serval *(Felis serval)*
Africa
Long legs help to give good visibility as the serval walks through grassland, while its tall ears and acute hearing serve to reveal the presence of rodents. When food is short, however, these wild cats will even eat grass. They are powerful jumpers, able to leap up to nearly 10ft (3m) from the ground. Young servals can be tamed quite easily, and purr readily when relaxed.

Flat–headed cat
(Felis planiceps)
Asia
Ranging from Thailand to the islands of Sumatra and Borneo, this species is believed to feed mainly on fish and other aquatic creatures. It has very sharp teeth and a flat, broad head.

Fishing cat *(Felis viverrina)*
Asia
Not averse to wading into shallow streams to catch passing fish, these small cats are characterized by their short tails, which account for less than a third of their total head and body length. The toes of their front feet are webbed, which could assist them to swim.

Rusty–spotted cat
(Felis rubiginosus)
Asia
About half the size of a typical domestic cat, this is the smallest member of the whole family, and largely nocturnal. Able to climb well, and frequently appears to hunt off the ground, raiding birds' nests and catching roosting birds.

Sand-dune cat *(Felis margarita)*
Asia, Middle East, and Africa
A true desert-dweller, with thick mats of fur on the soles of its feet. These help it to walk on sand without sinking, and also afford protection against the heat on the ground. Hunts at night, preying especially on desert rodents. Needs to drink very little water.

Black–footed cat
(Felis nigripes)
Africa
Found in the southern part of the continent, this is the smallest of the African *Felis* species. It has acquired a reputation for aggression. Young develop more rapidly than domestic cats at first, but they attain maturity much later — typically not until they are around 21 months old. Has hybridized with both domestic cats and African wildcats.

Small cats of the new world

Geoffroy's cat *(Felis geoffroyi)*
South America
The black spots on the coat of this species often form lines. These cats live solitary lives, inhabiting quite small territories which are typically just ¾–1 ⅕ sq. miles (2–3 sq. km) in area. Widely distributed in the southern part of the continent, they may occur at relatively high altitudes in the Andean region.

Ocelot *(Felis pardalis)*
North, Central, and South America
These wild cats range from the southern United States down to parts of Argentina, Paraguay, and Peru. Their markings are highly individual, and no two individuals look alike, but this has not protected them from being heavily hunted for their fur.

Margay *(Felis wiedii)*
Central and South America
Sometimes confused with the ocelot, but distinguishable by their smaller size and much longer tail, margays are well adapted to an arboreal life style. They are the only cats capable of running head first down a tree without losing their balance.

African wild cats

Africa is the continent where domestication of the cat began, and members of the family from small to large are represented there. Some inhabit forested areas, whereas others live in open plains.

1 African golden cat
2 Black-footed cat
3 Serval

Asian wild cats

Asia is home to the largest of all wild cats — the tiger. Unfortunately hunting and deforestation are having a harmful effect on wild cat populations.

1 Pallas's cat
2 Marbled cat
3 Leopard cat
4 Bornean red cat
5 Desert cat
6 Rusty-spotted cat
7 Iriomote cat
8 Fishing cat
9 Tiger
10 Clouded leopard
11 Jungle cat
12 Flat-headed cat
13 Snow leopard
14 Temminck's golden cat

Mountain cat
(Felis jacobita)
South America
This species is found in the Andes mountains, often above the snow line up to altitudes of 16,730ft (5,100m). Very little is known about its habits, although it is thought to prey on rodents such as chinchillas. It has a relatively long, dense coat, which presumably affords some protection against the biting cold of this region.

Oncilla
(Felis tigrinus)
South America
One of the smaller New World cats, this species is typically found in wooded areas. Little spotted cats are agile climbers, and may catch prey off the ground. They are highly aggressive, and have been known to kill domestic cats on occasion.

Jaguarundi
(Felis yagouaroundi)
North, Central, and South America
This wild cat has a distinctive appearance, looking more like a weasel than a cat. Its body is slender, with short legs, while its tail may be as long as 20in (51cm). There are two distinctive colors — the red variant used to be called the eyra, and was thought of as a separate species from the gray jaguarundi. It is now known that kittens of both colors can occur in the same litter.

Kodkod *(Felis guigna)*
South America
Confined to a small area on the southwestern side of the continent, the kodkod typically weighs around 4 ½ lb (2.1kg), which makes it the smallest of the New World wild cats. Two distinct races are recognized, one of which has black spots on its feet.

Puma *(Felis concolor)*
North, Central, and South America
The most widely distributed of the New World wild cats, the puma is significantly larger than other members of the *Felis* genus, weighing as much as 227lb (103kg). It is remarkably athletic, being capable of jumping nearly 40ft (12m) if threatened. It is not unknown for pumas to attack people but generally they are very shy cats.

Pampas cat *(Felis colocolo)*
South America
This species looks very similar to the European wildcats, lacking the black spotting associated with other New World *Felis* species. It is found not only in grassland areas but also in forested and upland areas. The hair running down the back is long, resembling a small mane in some cases.

The Lynx group

North American lynx
(Lynx canadensis)
North America
The numbers of this species, also called the Canadian lynx, are closely linked with those of its main prey — the snowshoe hare. Availability of food is the limiting factor in their harsh far-north habitat. In years when the hare population is high, the lynx numbers soar. Both follow a cyclical pattern extending over a period of nearly ten years, with the hare population falling before that of the lynx and then recovering sooner.

Spanish lynx *(Lynx pardinus)*
Europe
Restricted to a small area in the southwest of Spain and the adjoining area of Portugal, this species is endangered. It is smaller than the Eurasian lynx, and has a more heavily spotted coat.

Bobcat *(Lynx rufus)*
North America
Occurring farther south than the North American lynx, across the continental United States (south of Canada) down to southern Mexico, the bobcat is so called because of its short tail. Ear tufts are less prominent than in other lynxes, and may be totally absent in some cases. Young start hunting with their mother from the age of five months and start to split from the family group four months later.

Caracal *(Lynx caracal)*
Africa, Middle East, and Asia
The unusual name of these wild cats comes from the Turkish word *karakal*, meaning "black–eared." The rest of their coloration tends to a sandy brown. Caracals are exceedingly agile hunters.

Eurasian lynx *(Lynx lynx)*
Europe and Asia
The decline of the lynx in Europe has now led to attempts to reintroduce it to some of its former strongholds, such as parts of Switzerland. Compensation is paid to farmers for attacks on their stock, to discourage any further hunting of these wild cats. It is hoped this will enable them to increase their numbers again.

Big cats

Marbled cat
(Pardofelis marmorata)
Asia
Found in the southern part of the continent, these cats inhabit forested areas, and are agile climbers. In spite of their small size, averaging no more than 40in (102cm) long, these cats show a very close genetic relationship with the tiger. Pregnancy lasts 11 weeks. The characteristic marbling pattern on the coat develops after the young are around six and a half weeks old. They will have their adult markings by four months.

Onza *(not yet classified)*
Central America
Described by the early Spanish invaders of Mexico, but dismissed by zoologists, who believed such reports referred to pumas, this species finally had its existence confirmed on the night of January 1, 1986, when one of these cats was shot by a rancher. It weighed 60lb (27kg) and measured 68in (186cm), including its tail, which was 23in (73cm) long. The name "onza" comes from the Spanish word *uncia*, which means "cheetah" and refers to its relatively long legs.

Leopard *(Panthera pardus)*
Africa, Middle East, and Asia
A powerfully built large cat, the leopard is adaptable by nature, hunting both on the plains of Africa and in the forests of Asia. Will often drag its kill up a tree, where it will be out of reach of scavengers. Melanistic leopards are known as black panthers.

Lion *(Panthera leo)*
Africa and Asia
The Asian lion is now restricted to a very small area, in the Gir Forest of India. In the past, lions used to range across Africa to the shores of the Mediterranean and on through the Middle East to the Bay of Bengal, on the eastern side of India. The lion is the only true social cat, living in groups called prides, in which lionesses hunt together to achieve a kill. The size of a pride is influenced by the availability of prey; where hunting is good, prides are larger. Prides that have acquired man–eating tendencies can be extremely dangerous.

Jaguar *(Panthera onca)*
Central and South America
Frequently found close to rivers and sea shores, the jaguar can swim well, and will catch a variety of aquatic prey, ranging from turtles, whose shells it can crack with its sharp teeth, to caimans and snakes, even large anacondas. It has light areas in the center of its black spots.

Clouded leopard
(Neofelis nebulosa)
Asia
So-called because of their cloud–like markings, these wild cats have been heavily hunted for their attractive fur, and are now extinct in some parts of their former range, such as Taiwan. Deforestation remains a major threat to their future in many areas. Male clouded leopards grow faster and ultimately attain a larger size than females.

Snow leopard
(Panthera uncia)
Asia
Found in the far east of the continent, in inhospitable terrain, the snow leopard is well protected against the cold, with a dense, pale–colored coat which helps it to merge into the landscape. Hunts relatively large quarry, such as wild sheep and deer, but is equally capable of catching hares and birds.

Tiger *(Panthera tigris)*
Asia
These wild cats are instantly recognizable by their striped patterning. The Siberian race of the tiger is the largest wild cat in the world, weighing up to 700lb (320kg). Tigers tackle large quarry, and can represent a serious danger to humans in some areas. The tiger population has plummeted in recent years in spite of protection — tigers are illegally hunted for body parts used in a variety of oriental medicines.

Cheetah *(Acinonyx jubatus)*
Africa, Middle East, and Asia
Cheetahs are the sprinters of the cat family, capable of reaching speeds up to 62mph (100kph), which makes them the fastest land mammals. They are now virtually extinct in Asia. It is a hazardous life for young cheetahs at first; often they die from starvation soon after leaving the mother at around 15 months old. It can take them three years to become fully proficient hunters. Small antelopes such as gazelles are their major source of food.

American wild cats

The range of wild cats extends from the far north right down to the tip of South America, confirming the adaptability of this family. The secretive lifestyle of wild cats is shown by the case of the onza, which remained unrecognized by science up until 1986.

1 Puma
2 Jaguar
3 Spanish lynx
4 North American lynx
5 Jaguarundi
6 Little spotted cat
7 Mountain cat
8 Geoffroy's cat
9 Pampas cat
10 Margay
11 Kodkod
12 Bobcat
13 Ocelot

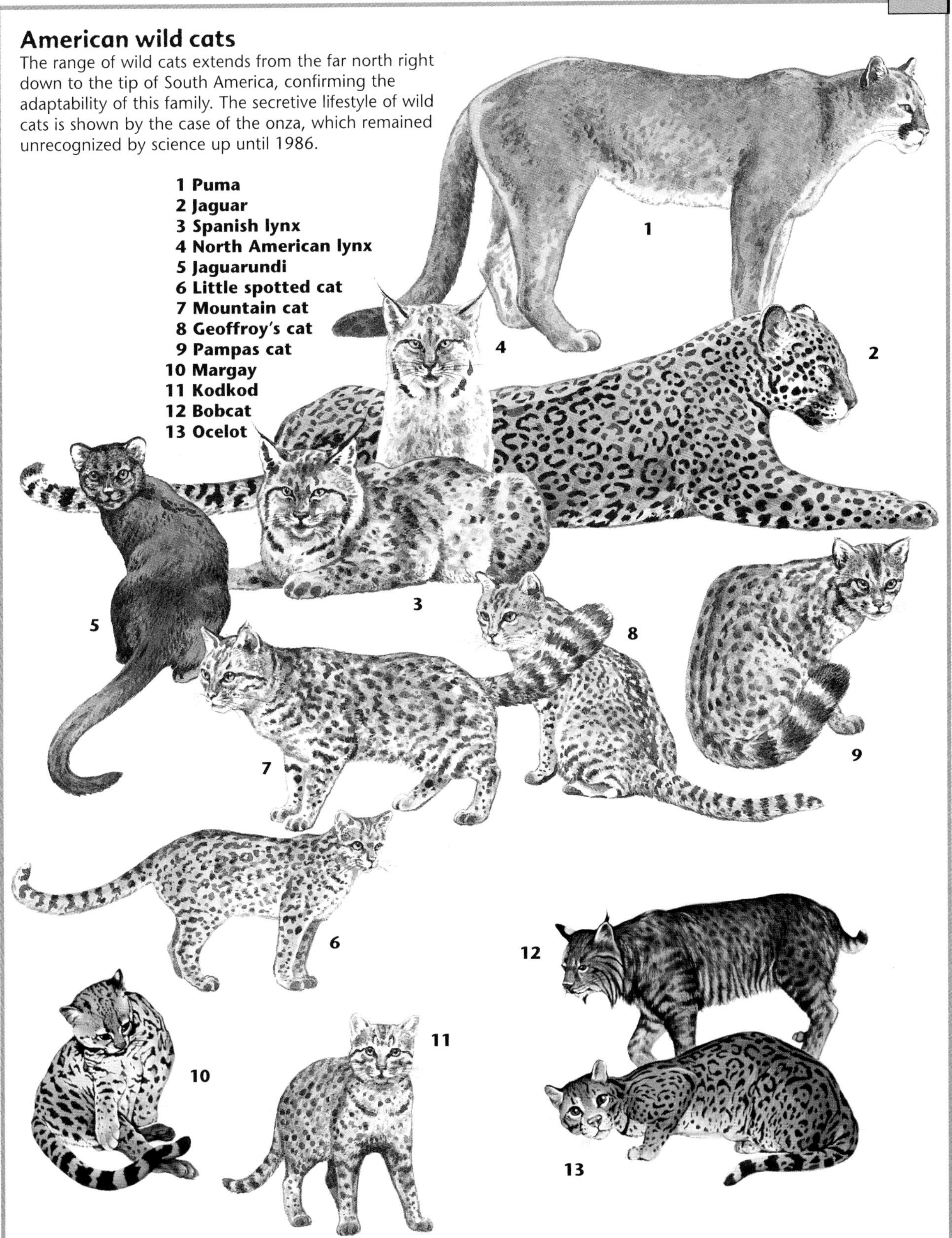

WILDCATS: THE CLOSEST COUSIN

The Wildcat's Habitat

The wildcat has a very wide distribution, being found as far north as Scotland and down through parts of southern Europe right to the tip of Africa. Eastward, its terrain extends throughout the Middle East and as far as western India and parts of the former USSR. Its range has contracted, however, particularly in Britain, where its distribution is now restricted to the far north.

The wildcat shows a striking resemblance to all the world's domestic cats, being their original ancestor. At first sight, it looks rather like a domestic cat with tabby markings. The wildcat does not occur in the Americas.

The reasons for the decline of the wildcat are various. These cats have been present in Britain for over two million years, and up until 500 years ago they were to be found across most of the country. Clearance of the forests that provided them with cover and plenty of opportunities for hunting small rodents did play a part, although wildcats have adapted to non-forested terrain in Africa and elsewhere.

Wildcats were also killed at every opportunity by gamekeepers, especially from the mid-1800s and up to the start of the First World War in 1914. They were regarded as vermin because they sometimes preyed on game birds. Tales among farming communities of these cats killing lambs are now thought to be mainly untrue, but such stories kindled further resentment against them.

Practical Pointer

Neutering cats not only helps to prevent unwanted kittens, including possible hybridization where wildcats are found in the same area. It also helps to prevent tomcats from straying off for long periods in search of possible mates.

Return of the wildcat

The wildcat population then underwent a temporary resurgence during the 1920s, as the great estates began to fragment, but by this stage the population was already restricted to Scotland. Hunting of these cats has still continued however, with estimates suggesting that several hundred were still being killed each year, even up to the 1980s. Subsequently, the decline of the Scottish wildcat led to the remaining population's being given complete protection in 1988.

The irony now is that the wildcat's domesticated descendant poses a potentially serious threat to its continued survival in Britain and other places where it lives close to human settlements. This is because of increasing hybridization, caused particularly by male domestic cats mating with wildcat females. Recent studies suggest that such pairings have probably been going on for years and that they may have contributed to the decline in numbers of wildcats in other parts of the country.

BASIC INSTINCTS • Size helps survival
The wildcat still has one of the most extensive ranges of all the non-domestic species of cat. Its relatively small size and shy nature, plus the fact that it poses no direct threat to humans, allow it to live unmolested, at least where it poses no threat to farm animals. The situation is very different for its larger wild cat relatives, such as tigers, which are now critically endangered because of human hunters. Wild cats in general face few threats from other predators.

Wildcat studies

The earliest reference to the problem of the hybridization between European wildcats and domestic cats comes in 1896, when a zoologist named Edward Hamilton recorded how, after examining the pelts of many so-called wildcats, he was convinced that domestic cat genes had become widely distributed through the wildcat population. For many years his findings were ignored, but now research has shown not only that wildcats will mate readily with domestic cats but also, more significantly, that the resulting offspring are themselves fertile and can breed successfully.

Investigations by a Polish zoologist, Pierre Suminski, have suggested that the typical so-called wildcat in Scotland is now only two-thirds pure, and that the situation is worsening, in spite of the fact that wildcat numbers appear to be increasing. Across Europe, according to Suminski, the wildcat has now become seriously affected by matings involving domestic cats, particularly in the vicinity of the Swiss and French Alps.

Suminski based his findings on studies of the different coat markings and of the skulls of specimens, noting that the purest population for which he had data was actually to be found in Poland itself, where the figure stood at 73 percent (purity of the wildcat lineage). The greatest hope for the survival of the true form of the wildcat is in remote parts of its range. The African population is probably purer, owing to the smaller proportion of domestic cats that are kept there.

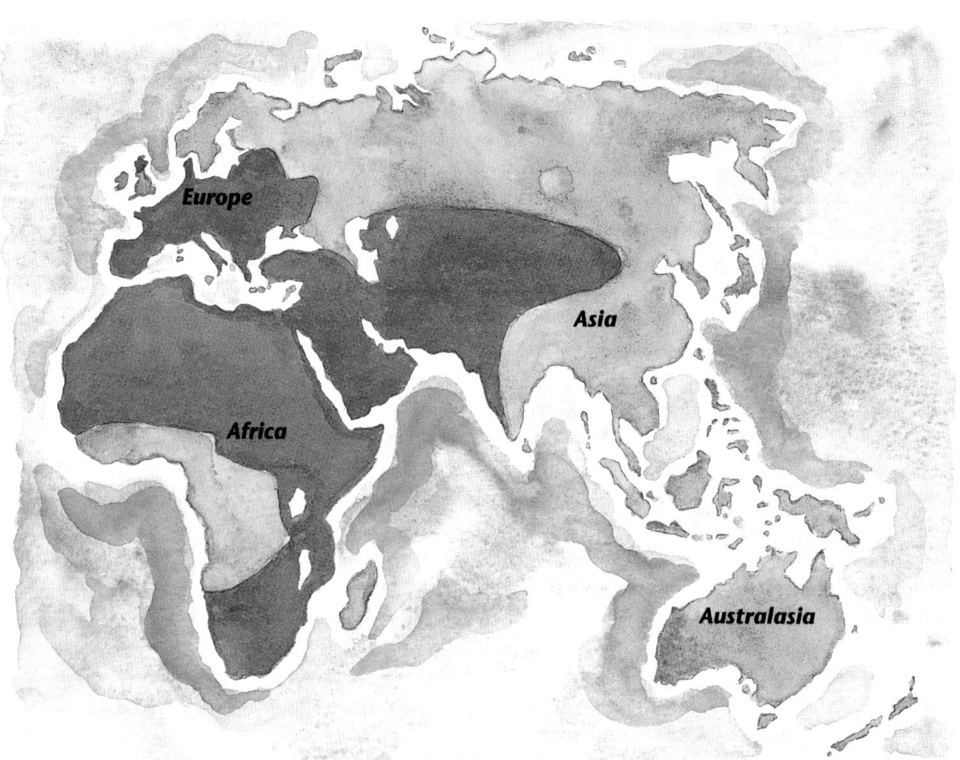

The wildcat has the widest distribution of any felid (indicated by red areas on map), ranging from northern parts of Europe down to the tip of southern Africa, and eastward through the Middle East into Asia. Within its range, a number of subspecies have been identified, with the African population from which the domestic cat was originally descended, sometimes being considered a separate species.

Opposite *Wildcats should not be confused with feral cats. These are domestic cats that have reverted to living and breeding in the wild; wildcats are a species not derived from domestic stock. Tabby markings may predominate in feral cats, as shown by these kittens. The appearance of wildcats is less variable.*

Practical Pointer

If you hope to see wildcats, you are most unlikely to come across them during the day, as they are shy by nature and tend to be nocturnal. In the winter, however, they may sometimes be spotted in daylight, having wandered from their dens searching for food.

Cat migrations

The European wildcats are generally more aggressive than those found in Africa. Clearly, one of the main attractions of keeping a domestic cat is that in spite of being more independent by nature than a dog, it will still be affectionate toward its owner and immediate family, even if somewhat withdrawn with strangers. Yet it does not take long for cats to revert to the ways of their wild ancestors.

The adaptability of feral cats probably stems in part from the wide area over which their wildcat cousins occur. Throughout their range, wildcats can be found in many different types of terrain. In Europe, they are most likely to be encountered in areas of deciduous or coniferous woodland, while in parts of Africa and Asia these cats are found even in arid, rocky landscapes where there is little vegetation. Their diet is equally varied, being influenced by the creatures found in the area where they are living.

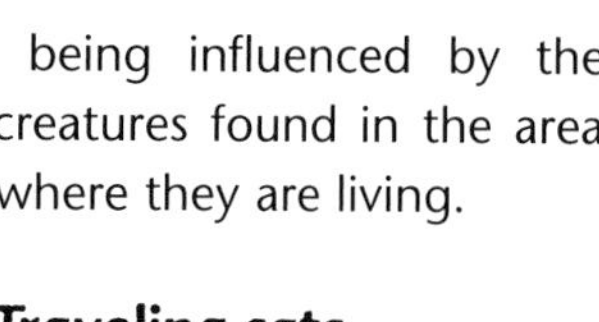

The Maine coon evolved in the USA from European domestic cats.

Traveling cats

The versatility of the cat, and particularly its ability to control rodents, gave it free passage on the long voyages of exploration, from the time of Columbus up until the nineteenth century. These animals were welcomed on board, and ships' cats were a common sight. A number of today's breeds trace their ancestry back to this period. The origins of the Maine coon cat, for example, lie in Portland, Maine, its ancestors having been brought there from Europe.

Unfortunately the legacy of this movement of domestic cats around the world has not been entirely benign, and the effects are still evident in some parts of the world today. Ships' cats often left their vessels "at port," with the result that over the centuries, in many places, cats remaining behind soon adopted the lifestyle of their ancestors and reverted to catching whatever prey was available.

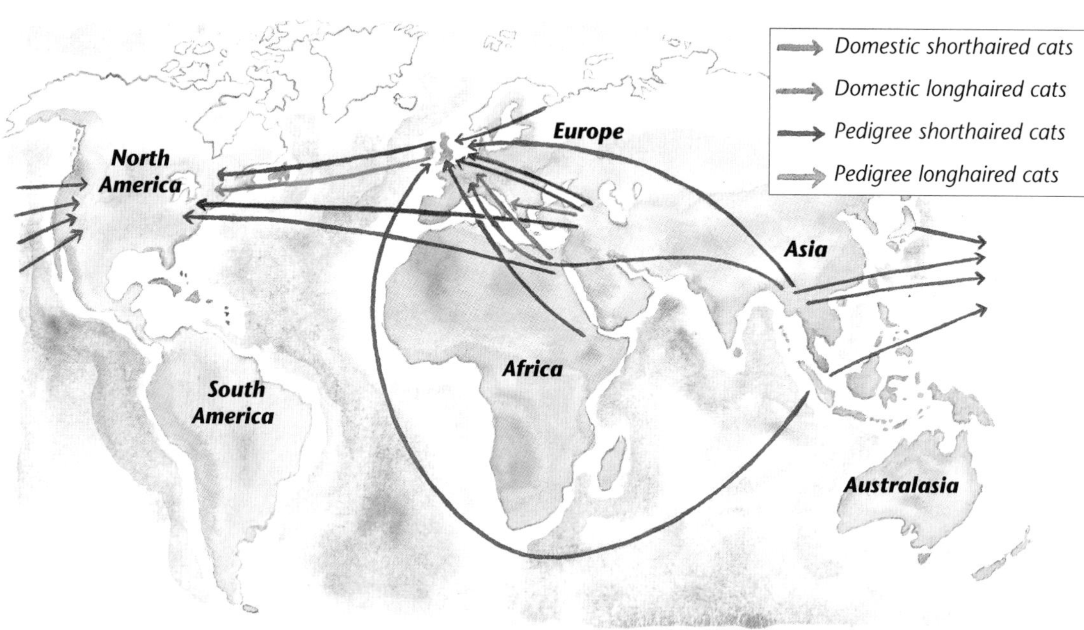

This map illustrates the worldwide spread of domestic cats, and also shows how breeds from both Europe and Asia (originally derived from wildcat lineage) were taken to North America over many centuries.

In some cases the effects on the local wildlife have been catastrophic — particularly on some remote islands. In the Galapagos Islands, off the western coast of South America for example, the descendants of cats brought there in the 1700s prey on a variety of the unique wildlife, ranging from the endangered dark-rumped petrel (*Pterodroma p. phaeopygia*) to newly hatched giant tortoises (*Geochelone elephantopus*) and marine iguanas (*Amblyrynchus cristatus*). They do have some positive impact, however, in controlling the black rat (*Rattus rattus*), also brought to the islands by visiting ships. Control of the cat population in such localities has become vital to the conservation of many unique creatures found nowhere else in the world.

Both feral and wildcat kittens prove aggressive by nature if cornered. They are very reluctant to accept human company.

European immigrants also brought cats with them when they began to make settlements in other parts of the world. In Australia for example, the first cats arrived with the initial wave of settlers in the late 1780s. Hunting in a landscape where there was no competition from other carnivores proved easy for them, and they soon spread across the continent.

It is in New Zealand, however, that feral cats have exerted a greater impact on the native wildlife than anywhere else in the world. Many of its endemic species, especially birds, ranging from the Chatham banded rail (*Cabalus dieffenbachi*) to the Stephens Island wren (*Xenicus lyalli*), have been totally wiped out by feral cats. The Stephens Island wren population was exterminated by the lighthouse keepers' cats in the early 1890s, before these birds were even officially known to science.

Practical Pointer

Always make sure that your cat comes in at night, rather than leave it outside roaming the streets. At this time it is more likely to come into conflict with feral cats and there is a possibility that it could be injured in a fight.

Cat control

Today, there are few major towns or settlements anywhere in the world that do not have a population of feral cats. These cats have reverted to living and breeding in the wild state and even their kittens are difficult to deal with, just like those of true wildcats. Welfare groups do not generally seek to rehome these cats. Instead the animals are caught humanely and neutered, then returned to the colony. By this means, the numbers of feral cats can be curbed and the population in controlled areas will ultimately die out naturally.

Markings

With wildcats occurring over such a wide area, it is not surprising to find distinctive variations in their appearance. These differences have been used by taxonomists to classify them into subspecies or races, although the validity of these is often a matter of intense debate. Some zoologists regard the European and African wildcats as subspecies, whereas others consider them to be separate species. In any case, the variation in appearance between wildcats from different areas gives a valuable clue as to how the range of coat markings seen today in domestic cats has arisen.

The fur of the wildcat in northern areas, where the winters can be very cold, is considerably longer than that of most domestic cats. The long guard hairs, which protrude through the softer, insulating down, may be over 2 inches (5cm) long. The coloration of European wildcats from the northern part of their range is relatively dark. The dark stripes contrast with a relatively grayish-brown coat, although the underparts are white. There may also be white fur around the mouth.

The pattern of the stripes varies among individuals, even from the same litter, as do the markings on the head.

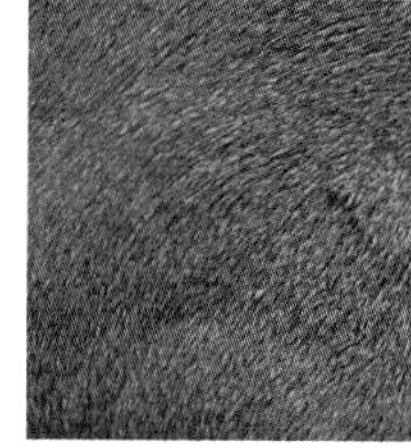

Ticked tabby

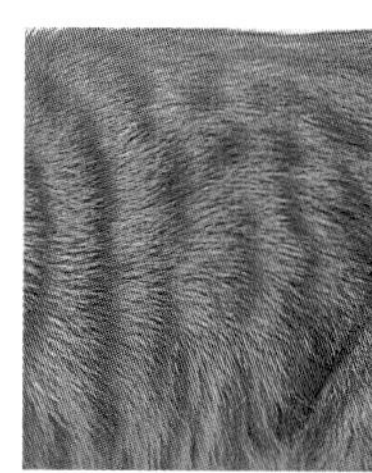

Mackerel tabby

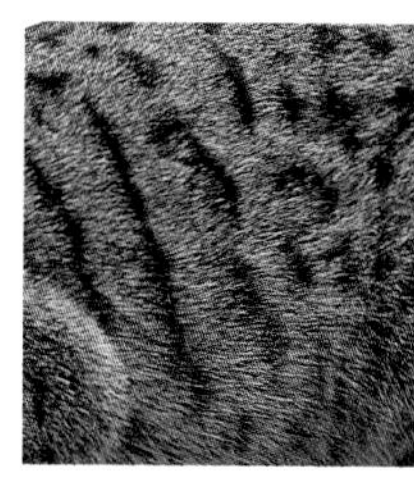

Spotted tabby

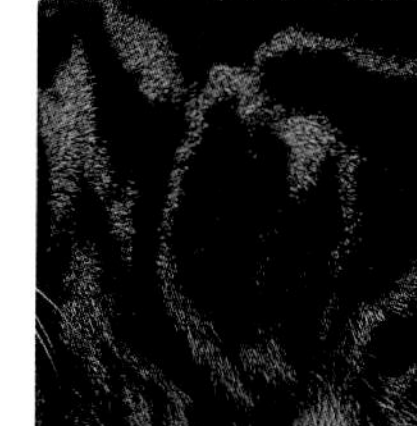

Classic tabby

These markings provide what is often described as disruptive camouflage, which is particularly effective in woodland or forested areas, where lighting conditions are poor. Here, the stripes serve to break up the cat's outline, helping to conceal its presence, especially when it is standing still.

How tabbies got their name

The striped and spotted pattern of markings found on wildcats has become known as "tabby." This name originates from the district of al Attabiya, in Baghdad, Iraq, which is famous for a particular type of washed black and white silk. This fabric was imported into Britain on a relatively large scale in the 1800s, becoming known as "tabbi-silk." As a result, cats with similar patterning began to be called tabbies.

Tabby markings remain dominant in domestic cats today. Most crossbreed cats still display stripes over at least part of their coat. Even in the case of single-color or pedigree cats, where a single color is bred for and expected, darker tabby areas are often evident, especially in kittens. These may disappear as the cat grows older. But those with the most pronounced tabby markings as kittens often develop into the best-colored adults, showing good depth of coloration.

Selective breeding has also been responsible for developing the tabby markings seen in wildcats into a very precise patterned arrangement. The markings that most closely correspond to the wildcat in appearance is the so-called mackerel tabby, which has narrow stripes running down each side of the body, creating an outline not unlike the outline of a fish. There are characteristic tabby rings around the tail and similar markings on the legs.

Blotched tabbies

An early variant on tabby patterning is the blotched or classic form, which arose around the eleventh century and has recently been selectively bred.

In this instance, the contrasting areas of dark fur and light fur are much more pronounced, being relatively large.

Practical Pointer

Tabby markings are most pronounced in shorthaired cats, regardless of whether or not they are of pedigree stock. This is because their fur is sleeker than that of longhairs, and so the markings are less blurred.

There are typically three broad sweeps on each side of the cat's body, complete with a so-called oyster pattern on each flank. Other distinguishing features are two broad, dark bands running parallel with a central thin stripe extending down the back.

Although the markings on the body may differ, breeders seek cats with markings that resemble the letter "M" on the forehead.

Black lines that sweep from the outer corners of the eyes and across the cheeks, known as mascara lines, are also considered desirable.

Such features are to be seen in non-pedigree cats as well, but they tend not to be clearly defined. They are also to be seen in the spotted tabby, where the lines are broken up into spots, that may vary somewhat in shape.

The ultimate form of tabby, in which virtually all the markings have been bred out, is the ticked or agouti coat, which is exemplified by the Abyssinian breed.

In this coat, there is no evidence of dark tabby bands or spots. Instead, the hairs have alternating light and dark bands along their length. Hints of this cat's tabby ancestry are the traces of markings still apparent on the head.

The so-called wild Abyssinian, a breed that came to prominence in the 1980s (see page 41), still retains distinctive dark necklaces and traces of barring on the legs, that are reminiscent of its tabby ancestors and demonstrate how today's Abyssinian would have looked at an earlier stage in its development.

BASIC INSTINCTS • Stripes not spots

The tiger is instantly distinguishable from all other species of wildcat by the stripes on its body. These provide good camouflage, serving to break up the tiger's outline, particularly in heavily forested areas, which tend to be this cat's natural habitat. The unique pattern of each tiger's stripes enables zoologists studying these wild cats to identify individuals. The patterning on young tiger cubs will remain consistent throughout their lives.

In the Abyssinian itself, dark areas of tabby markings have been removed from the coat by selective breeding.

ANATOMY OF THE CAT

The domestic cat today retains much of the agility of its wildcat ancestor, although it is generally smaller. Appearance can be deceptive, though, since long-haired domestic cats always tend to look larger than those with short hair because their hair stands away from the body. Still, wildcats from northern areas also tend to be heavier than those from southern Europe or Africa, for example. This is likely to be a reflection of their need to lay down fat reserves in their bodies in the late fall (autumn) to help them to survive the winter, when food is often difficult to obtain.

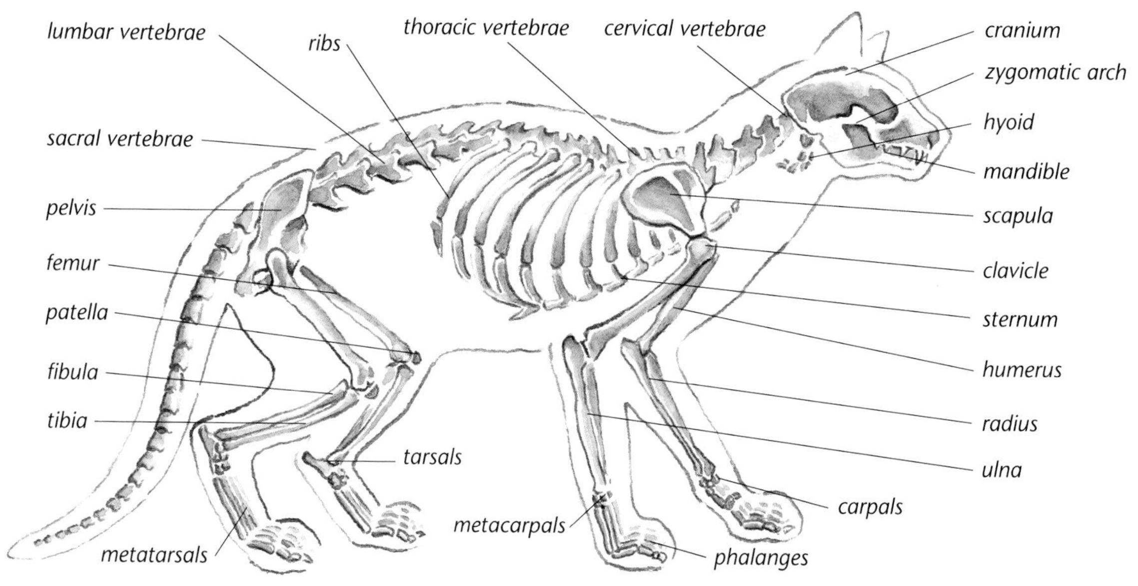

A cat's skeleton comprises approximately 244 bones, with discs between the vertebra as shock-absorbers.

Jaws and teeth

The skull of the wildcat is, on average, longer than that of the domestic cat, and the jaws are more powerful. The teeth, too — particularly the long pointed canines at the corners of the mouth — are larger, being up to ¾ inch (2cm) long in some cases, which makes the wildcat a formidable predator. The dentition of wildcats and domestic cats is otherwise identical. In common with most members of the cat family, both have a total of 30 teeth, 16 of which are in the upper jaw.

Practical Pointer

If a cat catches a mouse it will swallow it head first because the mouse is far less likely to stick in the throat if ingested in this way. Cats that hunt must be treated regularly for tapeworms (see page 113). They can also be at risk from certain poisons used to kill rodents, for example, so try to prevent such behavior.

The sharp pointed canine teeth used to subdue and kill their quarry are clearly seen in this Scottish wildcat.

Teeth for killing

The long, pointed canines are the most significant, in terms of the cat's ability as a hunter, because they provide the means whereby prey can be grabbed and killed. These teeth are specifically shaped to enable the cat to subdue its quarry, by penetrating through the neck region between the vertebrae, and severing the spinal cord. This makes cats very effective killers, although this instinct is sometimes suppressed in domestic cats (see page 78).

Amazingly, as the cat seizes and struggles with its prey, special pressure-responsive cells in the vicinity of the canine teeth appear to direct it to strike at the appropriate spot, rather than attempting to bite through bone, which could damage the canines. As a further precaution, the muscles of the cat's neck are arranged so as to absorb any possible jarring, should the cat encounter bone at any stage in the process, or when it is feeding.

Between the canines and the teeth located to either side there is a gap; this allows the canines to be fully embedded into the prey at the outset, to assist in the kill.

BASIC INSTINCTS • Killer touch

Cats are highly effective predators, thanks not only to their stealth and speed but also to the way in which they can dispatch their quarry effectively after catching it. This is particularly important for many bigger cats, because they hunt large, potentially dangerous prey on their own and thus are at great risk of being injured unless they can overpower and kill their quarry quickly. Although cats often fail to catch their intended victim, when they do succeed in catching it there is little chance of escape, and death is almost instantaneous.

Teeth for eating

The small incisor teeth at the front of the mouth are used to pull off feathers or skin. Then the highly specialized carnassial teeth come into play. These are the third upper premolar teeth and the first molars in the lower jaw, located on the other side of the gap between the canines. The jaws of the cat do not shift from side to side; any lateral movement would reduce the

Above *Domestic cats mimic the eating habits of their wild relatives, by tilting their heads to one side when using their carnassial teeth.*

power of the canines. Thus chewing or grinding food is not possible. Instead, the carnassials, which are sharp and elongated, act like scissors, cutting through flesh very effectively. Their shearing motion enables them to slice through bone.

Domestic cats rarely rely on their carnassial teeth, because their food is supplied in such a form that it can usually be consumed easily. But if they obtain a large piece of meat, for example, they will use this technique to pull off strips of it.

Cats adopt a characteristic posture when using these teeth, with the head tilted to one side and the piece of food hanging out of the mouth. This is because only one pair of carnassials can be used at a time, and the cat tilts its head to exert maximum force. The powerful masseter muscle, located in the lower jaw, aids in this task.

After a suitable piece of meat has been torn off, the cat will swallow it and then continue to use its carnassials to get another piece, until its appetite is satisfied or all food has been eaten.

The effectiveness of the carnassial teeth would be compromised if they were not powerful, which is why the enlargement of the masseter muscle is important. This is also reflected in the cat's skeleton, by the bowing and thickening of the zygomatic arch, running on each side of the skull beneath the eye sockets. It provides a greater area of attachment for the masseter, thus improving its strength.

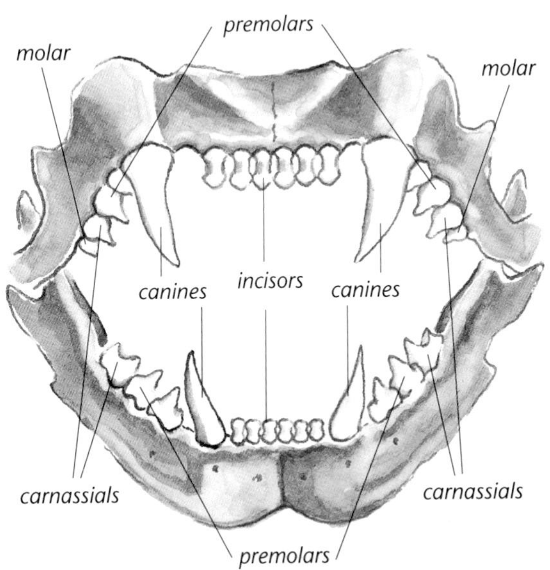

Above *The teeth of the cat are equipped for killing, with the sharp canine teeth at the front of the mouth being used to sever the spinal cord.*

Practical Pointer

If you are bitten by a cat, wash out the wound thoroughly and seek medical advice. There are usually bacteria present in the cat's mouth, and these are likely to cause an infection if injected into your flesh by a bite from the long canines.

Paws and claws

The cat's claws have an important part to play in its hunting technique. Not only do they provide extra support when climbing, but they are also used to grip and restrain prey. This can be particularly significant with wet prey such as fish, which form a major part of the diet of the Asian fishing cat. A firm grip also means it will be easier to dispatch the prey and lessens the risk of the cat itself being injured when tackling potentially dangerous quarry.

Another reflection of their hunting needs is the size of the feet. Wild cats have larger and more powerful feet in relation to their overall size than domestic cats. Both have the same number of claws, with four in contact with the ground on each front foot. The fifth, also called the dew claw, is located a short distance up the side of the foot. It is equivalent to the thumb, and often helps the cat to grip more securely when climbing, the paws being spread apart at this stage. Dew claws are missing from the hind feet of all cats.

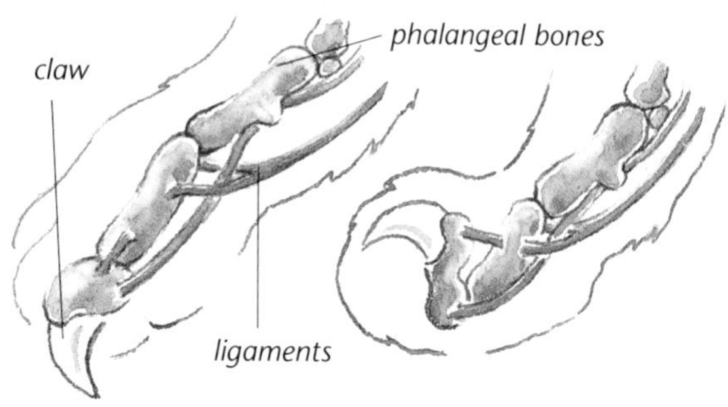

Most cats can withdraw their claws, which helps them to keep the tips sharp, rather than leaving them permanently exposed. This is done by an arrangement of ligaments that attach to the bones of the toes, enabling them to retract the claws when required.

A cat's claws are sharp and can be used for defensive purposes if necessary. For much of the time, however, they are carefully concealed by means of special ligaments which keep them protected, in a more vertical position. Cheetahs have a slightly different arrangement, linked in part to their specialized life style. They live on the plains of Africa, where there is little cover for hunting purposes. As a result, they rely heavily on their ability to outrun their prey. A cheetah's claws are permanently exposed — this a real advantage when the cat is running, as the claws provide additional support. A similar arrangement has been recorded in the case of the rare flat-headed cat, whose diet is thought to include a large amount of fish — in this case affording the cat greater agility.

The cheetah is the supreme athlete of the cat family. It is built for speed and cannot retract its claws. Its legs are also relatively long, giving good stride length.

Toe pads

The fleshy toe pads on the underside of cats' feet help to cushion them as the cat walks or climbs. In wildcats, they are pink at first in young kittens, and then turn black, while in domestic cats, the color varies. Those with white feet, such as the snowshoe breed, have pinkish pads. Although leathery to the touch, these pads will bleed profusely if cut, and this can happen if a cat jumps onto a wall with shards of glass embedded in the top.

Objects can also become stuck in the pads and work their way into the foot itself, which can prove very painful. This is most likely to occur in late summer, when grass stalks in fields are drying. Grass seeds not only can penetrate the foot, but also, with movement of the cat's muscles, track up the leg.

Another potential source of irritation to the foot is the harvest mite (*Trombicula autumnalis*), also known as a chigger. This is prevalent at the same time of year.

The adult form of this mite looks very much like a tiny red spider and does not cause any harm, since it does not have an animal host at this stage in its life cycle.

The problem is caused by the parasitic larvae, which attach themselves between the cat's toes and cause a great deal of discomfort. The cat will repeatedly lick at its feet in an attempt to relieve the irritation.

It is generally not wise to attempt to probe the foot pads when your cat is showing signs of distress in this area. It may be necessary to take the cat to the veterinarian to be sedated, so that the affected area can be thoroughly examined and possibly treated. Dealing with the mites is not problematical, but tracking a migrating grass seed will be more difficult, although a swelling on the leg can give an indication of its whereabouts.

Practical Pointer

Always check the feet of a cat or kitten carefully before purchasing it. The presence of extra toes — called polydactylism — is not uncommon, especially in Oriental breeds such as Siamese. Such cats do not appear unduly handicapped, but they should not be used for breeding purposes, nor can they be exhibited.

Practical Pointer

A cat that uses its claws to scratch itself repeatedly is likely to be suffering from fleas, so keep a close watch for such behavior. In some cases, a small number of fleas can cause great irritation.

Contrary to popular belief, cats rarely become stuck in trees, but they do find it harder to descend, and are forced to come down backwards. Their claws will help them to grip and climb the trunk without difficulty in the first instance.

Tails and whiskers

Cats rely on their tails as a counterbalance when they jump, and also as a means of communication. Annoyance, contentment, and fear can all be linked with movements of the tail. Most cats have a dark tip to their tails, which has a further function, particularly in the case of lions. As a group of hunting lionesses move through scrub, they may wish to be concealed, but it is equally important that they can see each other when deciding to strike. The tail provides a silent and relatively inconspicuous way of maintaining contact.

Cats are not afraid of jumping, and both wild and domestic cats will leap in a similar way, stretching out to absorb the impact with their front paws as they reach the ground again.

One of the main distinguishing features between wildcats and domestic cats is the appearance of the tail. In the case of a wildcat, the tail length may exceed 50 percent of its combined head and body length, but it will not be as long proportionately as that of most domestic tabby cats. The shape of the tail has also become modified as a result of domestication; it has become narrower as well as longer, while the dark markings are usually less distinctive.

Practical Pointer

It is quite normal for the whiskers of rex cats to be curled, and they are consequently shorter than normal. The whiskers may also be more fragile and tend to break off easily, especially in the case of the Devon rex, but they will regrow in time.

Variations on a tail

Siamese have particularly long tails, complementing their svelte bodies, but in this breed a genetic weakness producing kinked tails has arisen in some bloodlines. The problem is now less common, however, than it was formerly.

For many years following the introduction of this breed to the West, a kinked tail was deemed quite acceptable. In fact, the first Siamese awarded champion status in Britain had a noticeably deformed tail. It was said that these cats guarded rare vases in their native Thailand, curling their tails

Manx cats are not seriously handicapped by their short or missing tails.

around the handles, and that this was why they were kinked! Fortunately, breeders soon sought to eliminate this problem by careful breeding, so it is rare to see Siamese with misaligned vertebrae in their tails today.

The Manx is, of course, well known for its lack of a tail. Its spine is curved, however, because the vertebrae are shortened, with the result that these cats have a distinctive gait, not unlike that of a rabbit hopping along the ground.

In fact, only some Manx have no trace of a tail. These have been christened "rumpies" on their native island — the Isle of Man, off England's west coast. Those with short stubs of tails are called "stumpies," while Manx that have tails of almost normal length are referred to as "longies." In breeding Manxes it is important not to pair rumpies together. This is likely to result in a high incidence of birth defects, such as spina bifida, in the resulting kittens. Otherwise, Manx are often very long-lived cats, and appear to be able to climb quite effectively, even without a tail.

The cat's whiskers

Whiskers are specialist hairs arranged in groups on the cat's head. They are thicker than the guard hairs and have a sensory function. Whiskers will enable a cat to determine whether it can slip through a hole in a fence, for example, and they also respond to movement in its vicinity. The main group of whiskers is arranged on each side of the face, between the upper jaw and nose, with others above the eyes and just below the eyes on the sides of the head. Domestic cats have relatively long whiskers — an indication of their nocturnal habits. Wild cats that are active primarily during the day, such as cheetahs, have shorter whiskers. When the pupils are fully dilated, to capture as much light as possible in the dark, the eyes cannot focus easily at close quarters. This is when domestic cats are especially dependent on their whiskers. Cats without whiskers, particularly the mystacial whiskers on the side of the face, may have difficulty in finding their way in the dark.

Cats can weave through surprisingly narrow gaps without any difficulty, thanks to their whiskers which help them to assess whether the space is wide enough for them to squeeze through.

Practical Pointer

Stud tail is a problem found in cats of both sexes, although it is most common in unneutered males. It is caused by an excessive output from the sebaceous glands at the base of the tail. The area then becomes infected, with pustules developing. Washing the affected area with a suitable antiseptic may help, although antibiotics will be required to treat more severe cases.

THE SENSES

As hunters, cats rely heavily on their senses to locate prey and must depend on their sensory input in order to make a kill. If the cat leaps too soon, it will alert its quarry, which is then likely to escape. Cats have particularly acute hearing and vision, and they are less dependent on their sense of smell for hunting than many other carnivores. This may seem strange, in view of their nocturnal habits, but vision is the most important factor when they are timing a successful leap.

The appearance of a cat's eyes are affected by the prevailing light conditions. In a bright light, the pupils are reduced to slits as shown here.

In relative darkness, the cat's pupils are dilated to allow more light to enter and stimulate the cells on the retina.

Eyesight

The cat's eyes are well adapted for detecting and relaying information in lighting conditions that to our eyes would seem impossible. Their large eyes, located on the front of the head, give good visibility ahead. The pupils, through which light enters, can alter dramatically in shape, depending upon the prevailing light. They narrow to slits in bright light, and become much larger and circular in the dark. This ensures that as much light as possible enters the eye to create an image on the retina.

A further refinement is the *tapetum lucidum*, which forms a reflective layer up to 15 cells deep at the rear of each retina, and can be compared to a mirror. Light passing through the retina is directed back by these cells, stimulating the receptors in the retina itself. This is why cat's eyes shine brightly at night, when picked up in headlights, for example.

Rods and cones

As in human eyes, the cat's retina contains two types of cell: Cones and rods. Cones are sensitive to bright light, and rods respond best to dim light. While we have around four rods to each cone, the cat has 25 rods to each cone. With relatively few cones, the cat has poor color vision, but color does not seem to play an important part in their lives.

The way in which light enters the cat's eyes also helps the animal to see. The outer cornea is quite strongly curved. This creates a larger anterior chamber in front of the lens, which is also relatively curved. As a result, the retina is positioned closer to the lens, and the light here is more focused, helping to trigger a higher proportion of the rods, and so create a clearer image. This curvature of the cornea is less apparent in those species of wildcat, such as lions, that are active during the day than it is in the domestic cat.

BASIC INSTINCTS • Seeing at night

Although a dangerous predator, a tiger could itself be badly injured by its prey if it mistimed its leap. Its binocular vision enables the tiger to judge where to jump with great accuracy, so that it can knock its quarry off-balance and inflict a fatal bite. The *tapetum lucidum* at the back of each eye, which helps the tiger to see at night, can create an eerie glow when the tiger encounters a bright light, as shown here.

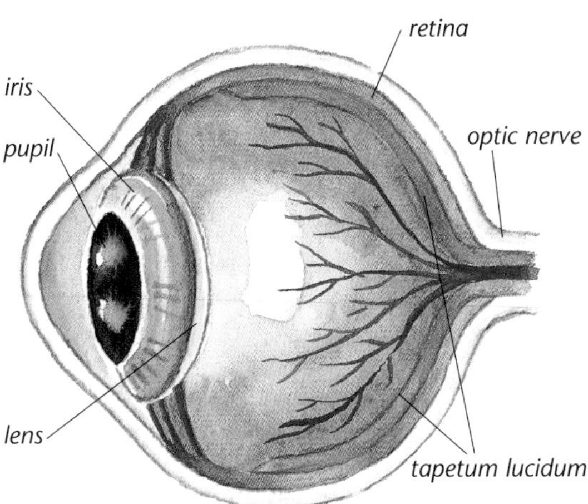

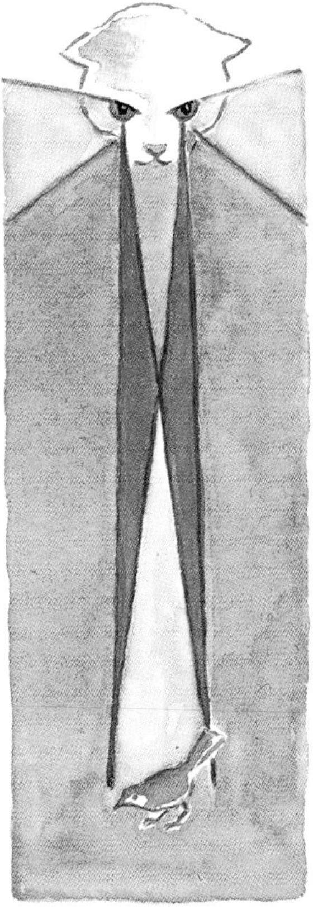

Left *Like other predatory mammals, including humans, cats have evolved binocular vision, which is vital to success in hunting. The image registers on the retina of each eye, and is conveyed to the cat's brain via the optic nerve (see diagram far left). The two separate images overlap slightly, enabling the cat to judge the position of its prey with great accuracy. This is not as well developed in some breeds, such as the Siamese, with the result that their hunting abilities can be compromised.*

Hearing

The hearing of cats is very sensitive, and far superior to our own. In smaller species such as the wildcat, this is partly a reflection of their prey. They can detect noises emitted by rats and mice in the high-frequency band, or ultra-sound, which is inaudible to our ears. Most cats can hear any sounds between 200Hz and 70Khz, but, as with humans, their ability to detect the upper frequencies declines notably with age.

The shape of the cat's external ear flaps, together with their mobility, can assist in locating the source of a sound extremely accurately. The serval, a wildcat which frequents areas of tall grassland, has particularly tall ears which may help it to track where

Above *Changes to the ear shape have arisen as a result of domestication, as in the case of the Scottish fold.*

Practical Pointer

Deafness is sometimes a problem in blue-eyed white domestic cats. A congenital malformation causes the organ of Corti, the main sound receiving part of the inner ear, to be nonfunctional, which blocks the passage of the sound waves to the auditory nerve, causing deafness. Such cats are at greater risk from traffic, especially in towns, and obviously do not respond to their owners' voices.

Left *The American curl has its ear cartilage twisted, but its hearing remains unaffected.*

rodents are hiding. Variations to the ear shape have occurred as a result of domestication. The Scottish fold has ears which are folded downward, while the American curl has wavy ears — neither breed appears at all handicapped by this change.

BASIC INSTINCTS • Self-reliance

The practice of hunting alone places a number of constraints on a predatory species. If the cat is not quick enough, losing the element of surprise too soon, its prey will escape. The uncertainty of the outcome also makes it important to be able to adapt in the face of unexpected movement by potential quarry. A combination of excellent sensory input and rapid reflexes makes cats highly effective hunters in a wide variety of environments.

Below *Broad, rounded ears help wildcats, such as this leopard cat, to locate the source of sound waves effectively.*

HYBRIDS

Union of Species

The mating of two different species of cat, such as a wildcat and a domestic cat, may possibly result in the production of hybrid offspring. The kittens of the union of different species of cats could show characteristics from both parents, although in some cases the offspring will exhibit the characteristics and bear a stronger resemblance to one parent than to the other.

It is not just the small wildcats that can breed together to produce hybrid offspring. This is a "liger" — a cross between a lion and a tiger, at Khartoum Zoo, Egypt.

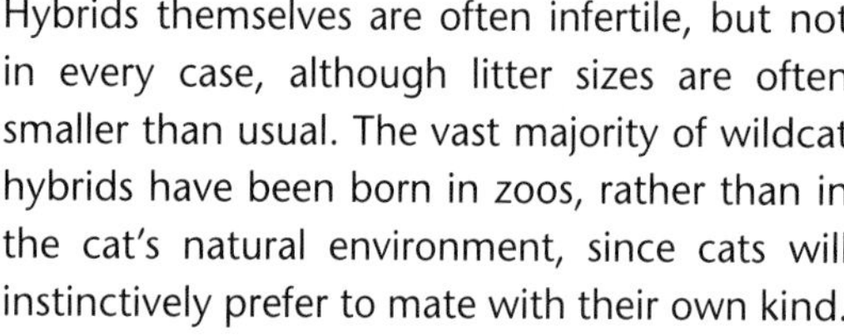

Hybrids themselves are often infertile, but not in every case, although litter sizes are often smaller than usual. The vast majority of wildcat hybrids have been born in zoos, rather than in the cat's natural environment, since cats will instinctively prefer to mate with their own kind.

It is not possible to predict the appearance of hybrid offspring when there is a wide difference between those of their parents. In the case of the so-called "leopon," a cross between a leopard and a lion, the pattern of spotting can be varied. The male offspring may display the mane of the lion and the head of a leopard.

A more common cross is between a lion and a tiger. The male's name is written first, so the result of a male lion mating with a female tiger is called a "liger," while that of a male tiger and a female lion is a "tigron." As already stated, such offspring are usually infertile, but there have been exceptions. At the Munich Zoo, the mating of a liger and lion did produce a cub. A jaguar x leopard hybrid also produced offspring when paired with a lion at the Chicago Zoo.

Wildcat – domestic cat offspring

In the case of wildcat–domestic cat hybrids, the situation is different because the domestic cat is descended from the wildcat. They are therefore far more closely related genetically than a tiger and lion, for example, and also still share many behavioral characteristics. It is not surprising therefore that they will mate and are capable of producing fertile offspring.

Studies carried out on captive stock and on those from the wild indicate that the wildcat appearance tends to be dominant in the offspring produced from such pairings.

Subtle changes, such as a slight decline in size and tapering of the tail are apparent however, and blotched black markings on the tail are also more common than among wildcats. Nevertheless, not all such pairings produce offspring with wildcat coloration.

Mike Tomkies, who has carried out detailed research into Scotland's surviving wildcats, has described how a female that he had released into the wild, mated with a black feral tomcat subsequently produced black and white offspring.

Cats with such conspicuous coloring may be more vulnerable to predators than a tabby-patterned hybrid or the wildcat itself. If seen in the wild, such cats would be identified as feral, rather than wildcat hybrids. In fact, an increase in the number of supposed feral cats could actually be indicative of growing hybridization in the wildcat population.

Hybrids produced from the mating of European wildcats with domestic cats are typically unfriendly, although not as hostile as pure wildcat kittens. This provides further evidence to support the theory that domestication began with the African rather than the European wildcat. In fact, while the European subspecies avoids human contact, its African relative is often encountered in the vicinity of human settlements, and appears to be much more amenable to contact with people. Before long, DNA studies will probably allow an accurate analysis of the relationships of the wildcat with the domestic cat, as well as unraveling the extent of hybridization in the wild population.

BASIC INSTINCTS • Keeping apart

Hybridization is a very rare occurrence in the case of wildcats, even where more than one species ranges through the same territory. One of the highest densities of wildcat species anywhere in the world is found on the island of Sumatra, off the coast of southeast Asia. Seven of the world's species live here, in addition to domestic cats; nevertheless, there is no evidence of cross-breeding among these types.

Zoologists believe that this may be because of the distinctive lifestyles of the different cats. Each has evolved a separate niche, so that they do not come into contact with each other, and can co-exist independently in a small area. The clouded leopard, for example, is a forest-dwelling arboreal species, feeding mainly on primates and birds, whereas the small Asian golden cat hunts smaller creatures in the treetops. Only where the wildcat population is small, as in Scotland or on the Japanese island of Iriomote, is hybridization likely to occur, in this case, between wildcats and their domestic cousins. It has been suggested that the long-coated Pallas's cat introduced the longhaired characteristic to domestic cats but it is more likely that it arose as a distinct mutation.

Hybrid breeds

Interest in incorporating the often-striking fur markings of wildcats into domestic cat bloodlines is not a recent phenomenon. It can be traced back to the origins of the cat fancy from the 1880s. In fact, there were special classes for such hybrids, and records suggest that up to ten of the smaller wildcats have been used at various times in the past in pairings of this type. It is not clear why none of these hybrid offspring was used to form the basis of a new breed. In fact, the idea of hybridization appears to have fallen out of favor up until the 1960s, possibly because of the rapid increase in the number of new cat varieties that were being developed by other means. Today, the breeding of small wildcats with domestic cats is considered unethical by the cat fancy.

Although it is bred to resemble a miniature black panther, the Bombay breed is derived entirely from domestic cat stock.

The Bombay cat

Some breeders did seek to create breeds based on the appearance of larger cats. Among them was Nikki Horner, of Kentucky, who pioneered the breed now called the Bombay. Her aim was to produce cats that resembled miniature black panthers (see picture left). She began by crossing a sable Burmese with a black American shorthair.

The jet black coat of the Bombay is short and sleek, which serves to emphasize the muscular, lithe profile of this breed. The eye color of kittens is blue at first, as in all cases, before changing through shades of gray to deep copper.

Practical Pointer

The Bengal is currently one of the most expensive breeds of purebred cat. Breeders have placed considerable emphasis on ensuring that their temperament is sound.

The California spangled

Another domestic breed created in a wildcat image is the California spangled, which, as its name suggests, originates in that state. It was created by a Hollywood scriptwriter named Paul Casey, who had been inspired by leopards he had seen on a visit to Africa. The spotted patterning was achieved by careful breeding over the course of five generations, using a variety of pedigreed and non-pedigreed breeds, including street cats obtained in Cairo, Egypt. The spots themselves are very well defined, while the body is long and muscular, which again corresponds to that of a wildcat.

The California spangled was originally advertised in a mail-order Christmas catalog of a famous store, and attracted considerable publicity as a result. It was Paul Casey's intention to use the breed to publicize the problems faced by many wildcats — both large and small — as the result of habitat decline, poaching, and other factors. Even now, California spangled kittens are highly sought after, to the extent that there is usually a waiting list for them.

Right *Many of the smaller wildcats such as the leopard cat can hybridize with domestic cats, although litter sizes may be smaller than normal. This species played a part in the development of the Bengal breed.*

The ocicat

By contrast, the ocicat is a breed with a wild cat appearance which arose from a chance mating between a chocolate point Siamese and an Abyssinian-seal point Siamese cross in Michigan in 1964. Their owner, Virginia Daly, was struck by the kitten's markings, which resembled those of the ocelot, a North American species whose northerly range extends to Arizona, south-western Texas, and New Mexico. The name of the breed is a combination of the words ocelot, accident and cat, reflecting both the appearance and the unplanned liaison that gave rise to this breed.

The Bengal

At present, however, the only breed that has been created by deliberate hybridization with a wildcat is the Bengal. Its origins can be traced back to the 1960s, when an American geneticist paired a male domestic cat with an Asian leopard cat that had been imported from Malaysia. Only one kitten resulted. This was fostered to a colorpoint Persian female and was reared with her litter. When mated back to her father in due course, this hybrid kitten produced both solid-colored and spotted offspring.

Serious development of these cats into the distinctive breed of today began in 1981, when Jean Mill acquired a group of eight female hybrids from fellow geneticist Dr. Willard Centerwall. At first the male cats were found to be infertile, but now this problem has been overcome, and these cats have attracted considerable interest among cat fanciers worldwide. The pattern of spots is very different from that of a spotted tabby, being aligned horizontally, and a striking similarity to the Asian leopard cat has been maintained in this breed.

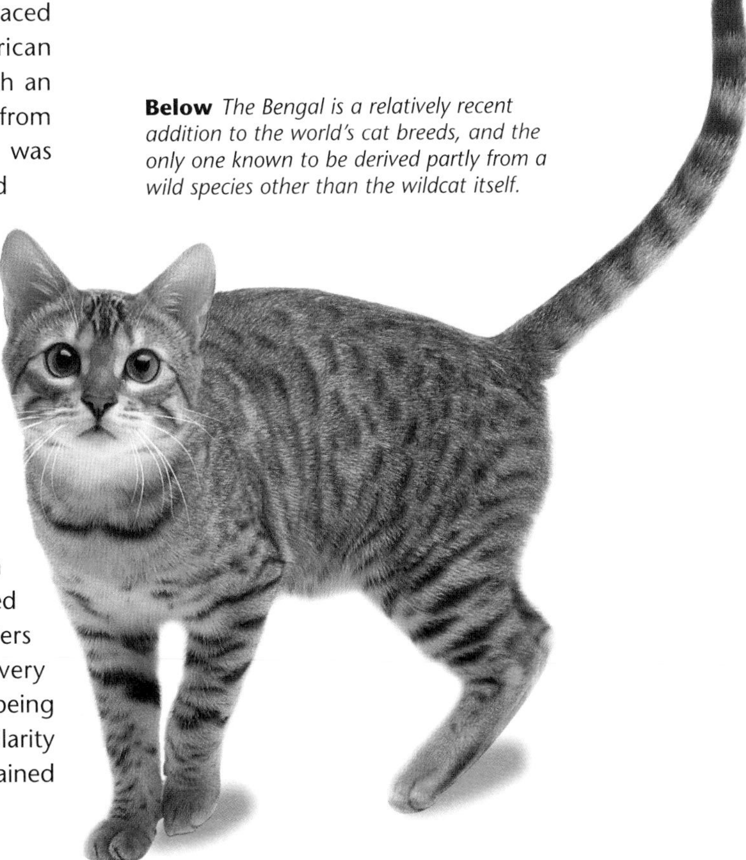

Below *The Bengal is a relatively recent addition to the world's cat breeds, and the only one known to be derived partly from a wild species other than the wildcat itself.*

DOMESTICATION

Exotic Ancestors

Although the origins of the domestication of the cat are unclear, it seems fairly certain that this occurred in Egypt more than 5,000 years ago. The earliest representations of cats may show wild individuals, but there is one of a cat fitted with a collar, which suggests evidence of domesticity. It dates back to 2600 B.C. From this stage onward, cats are increasingly portrayed in domestic surroundings, even helping their owners to catch waterfowl in the swamps of the Nile delta in one scene.

Pure colored cats such as this black British shorthair, called "selfs," have resulted from selective breeding.

Before long, the value of domestic cats in controlling rodents made them highly valued. In Egypt, a cult grew up around the cat and as many as 700,000 people would attend the annual festival of the cat goddess, Bastet, held in the city of Bubastis. Domestic cats were themselves considered sacred, and killing one was an offense punishable by death.

Their export to other countries was forbidden, but many cats did roam abroad, probably thanks to Phoenician sailors who traded around the shores of the Mediterranean and farther afield. Nevertheless, the Egyptians employed agents to travel and purchase cats in neighboring countries so that they could be taken back to their homeland.

Neither the Greeks nor the Romans fell under the spell of the cat to the same extent as the Egyptians. This may have been partly due to the fact that they relied on domestic ferrets for controlling vermin and so were less appreciative of the cat's hunting skills.

However, it was probably the Romans who introduced domestic cats to other parts of

Practical Pointer

The appearance of breeds is governed by their show standards, with breeders aiming to produce cats that will correspond as closely as possible to the perceived ideal. Cats that fail to meet these high standards, but are otherwise in good health, can still make excellent pets.

Europe; it is likely that they were established by the fourth century A.D. They probably followed the Silk Road, via the Middle East to China.

World travelers

In China, cats were valued not only for their vermin-killing ability, but also as symbols of good fortune. In India, the maternity goddess Sasht was endowed with feline form. It is still possible in part to trace the routes along which the domestic cat spread, by studying the cat populations in different countries today. Around the Mediterranean, which could be viewed as the domestic cat's next stop after Egypt, there is still a preponderance of tabbies among the feral populations. These cats bear a strong resemblance to those portrayed in the murals of ancient Egypt, displaying a clear relationship to the African wildcat itself.

The orange-red coloration of some domestic cats today first arose in the region of Asia Minor. The Vikings appear to have played an important part in distributing cats of this color, not only through Scandinavia but also to the far north of Britain and possibly Brittany, in France, too.

The tabby pattern now known as the classic or blotched form emerged around A.D. 1000. Its route through Europe follows the vital river routes, down the valleys of the Rhône and Seine in France, back to the Mediterranean.

It is not clear if the eastern populations of the wildcat played a part in the development of domestic cats in Asia, although this may well have been the case. The coats of cats originating in this part of the world are very different from those found in Scandinavia, for example, lacking a dense undercoat in the case of the Siamese and other breeds from this area.

Practical Pointer

It is commonly believed that ordinary crossbreeds are healthier than purebred cats, but both are equally vulnerable to the killer viruses that can afflict cats. All cats should be vaccinated regularly to protect them from such illnesses.

Early longhairs

The emergence of the longhaired characteristic is also rather controversial. It has been suggested that crosses involving another species of wild cat, known as Pallas's cat, may have contributed to this coat type, but this view tends to be dismissed today.

Pallas's cats were discovered during the 1700s by the German naturalist Peter Pallas, close to the Caspian Sea. He noted how these cats hybridized with domestic cats and suggested that this had led to the development of long-haired cats in Turkey. Pallas's cat has a longer coat than other wild cats and also small ears, a stocky appearance, and a broad head — all features associated with today's Persian longhairs. It also appears to be far more friendly than the European wildcat; individuals have been kept as pets and are well disposed to those whom they know well.

Bicolored cats are common, but for show purposes, the proportion of colored and white areas in the coat are well defined.

Modern breeds

The appearance of breeds today differs considerably from that of their ancestors. In the case of Siamese, for example, the head shape has become much more angular as the result of selective breeding, while the coat of the Persian longhair has become far more profuse. These changes have been brought about by selective breeding, which has also led to the development of a much wider range of color varieties.

At present there are almost 50 breeds, and many hundreds of accompanying color variants in some of these, such as the Oriental shorthair group. It has been calculated that there are more than 400 different possibilities that could be created.

Conversely, the coloration of some breeds is a highly distinctive feature, with only one color existing. The Korat, named for the province in northeastern Thailand where it was bred, is an example. Its appearance and coloration have remained essentially unchanged for centuries. Its blue coat has a very distinctive silvery sheen.

Persian longhair

Devon rex, with Siamese markings, often called a Si-rex.

Within the cat fancy there are changing fashions: Some breeds and even colors become popular for a period, and then decline in their appeal. But two of the original breeds — the Persian longhair and the British shorthair — still attract a strong following among cat lovers around the world. New colors have been introduced, such as chocolate and lilac, adding variety to these groups.

How breeds are developed

Breeds can be developed in several ways. First, there may be a spontaneous mutation that crops up unexpectedly, as happened with the Cornish rex. A kitten showing the usually curled or wavy coat associated with this breed appeared in the English county of Cornwall in 1950. By a careful breeding program, it was possible to develop the mutation so that it became well established, and the Cornish rex is now represented in many countries around the world. All such cats ultimately trace their ancestry back to that first kitten of the breed, named *Kallibunker.*

Other coat variants, including the hairless Sphynx breed, have evolved in a similar way, but more commonly breeds are developed by crossing two existing breeds. The introduction of pointed markings into the longhair bloodline for example, which ultimately gave rise to the breed now recognized as the colorpoint longhair, or Himalayan, began in this way. A black Persian longhair crossed with a Siamese were the founders of this most popular breed.

The third way in which breeds can be developed is by fixing the features of non-pedigree cats into a bloodline. This has given rise to the Singapura, for example, which is the smallest breed of domestic cat, typically weighing less than 6lb (2.7kg). It is descended from a group of feral cats obtained in Singapore in 1974 and taken to the United States, where the breed has since become very popular.

More recently, the wild Abyssinian cat has been developed in a similar fashion. The forerunners of this breed were also obtained in Singapore, with its subsequent evolution occurring in the United States in the 1980s. The Singaporean cats are noticeably larger than the Abyssinian itself, and have clear tabby barring (striped markings), mainly on the legs and tail.

Another similar emergent breed is the Ceylonese, whose homeland is the island of Sri Lanka (formerly known as Ceylon) off the coast of India. It is now being championed overseas, particularly in Italy.

Black and white Sphynx. The color results from skin pigmentation in this essentially hairless breed.

The evolution of cat breeds will continue. One of the most controversial today is the munchkin, a short-legged breed originally shown in the United States in 1991.

There are fears that its greatly reduced limbs could prove a handicap, while the joints could be more vulnerable to arthritis, although this is not a view shared by all cat fanciers.

Freedom from the need to hunt its own food has already produced alterations in the appearance of the domestic cat.

The bright coloration and patterning of many of today's pet cats is far removed from the subdued camouflage of their wild ancestors.

Singapura, the smallest cat breed in the world.

Practical Pointer

The appearance of kittens can differ markedly from that of adult cats. Their coats are much shorter, in the case of longhairs, while the point coloration will take time to develop in Siamese breeds and other breeds that have similar markings.

EARLY

LIFE

The breeding behavior of cats is unusual and is thought to be a direct reflection of their usually solitary lifestyles. When a pair do come together, there is every likelihood that pregnancy will occur, since the act of mating itself triggers ovulation, enhancing the possibilities for fertilization of the ova. This is in contrast to the situation with most other mammals, where ovulation takes place at a set time, rather than being caused by mating.

In domestic surroundings, where cats are living in much greater densities than in the wild, this almost inevitably means that a queen that is not spayed will soon become pregnant, thus increasing the numbers of unwanted kittens that are born every year. Think carefully before acquiring a cat, because it is a real responsibility, and be prepared to have your pet neutered at the appropriate time to avoid adding to this surplus population.

BREEDING

The Breeding Cycle

The breeding cycle of wild felines is closely geared to producing young at the most favorable time of the year. In the case of the European wildcat, living in the Northern Hemisphere, mating occurs in the early spring, so that the birth of the kittens will take place during the summer when prey is likely to be more plentiful. The domestic cat, which is generally far less dependent today than in the past on obtaining its own food, has a breeding period similar to that of its wild relative, although often somewhat longer.

Exposure to daylight appears to be the main factor controlling reproductive activity. In fact, cats housed permanently indoors and receiving at least 12 hours of light each day will continue to have reproductive cycles through most of the year. In cats without this constant light exposure there is usually a decline from the autumn to midwinter. This is the so-called anestrus period. Thus, in the Northern Hemisphere mating activity starts in January and extends roughly to September. Cats in the southern part of the world will commence breeding in October and continue until the following June. Those closer to the equator, where day length does not vary significantly, may have kittens at any stage of the year.

Finding a mate

One of the problems that all wild cats, except lions, have to face is finding a mate. (Lions live in groups called prides, with an adult male, several adult females, and some young animals.)

This problem arises because of the wild cats' solitary lifestyles. The same applies to domestic cats, so cats have evolved many ways in which contacts can be made.

Scent plays an important part. In addition to the nose, cats possess another means of detecting smells in the form of Jacobsen's organ — also known as the vomeronasal organ. This is located in the roof of the mouth and is especially sensitive to chemicals known as pheromones. These are present in the cat's urine and may be wafted on air currents. Pheromones will indicate the readiness of a female to mate and can attract males over a considerable area.

Cats of both sexes will spray their urine on prominent sites, such as tree stumps or fence posts, especially during the mating period. Another cat passing is likely to sniff the spot, curling its upper lip in a characteristic gesture called "flehmening." They are passing the scent molecules over the Jacobsen's organ and detecting the sex hormones present.

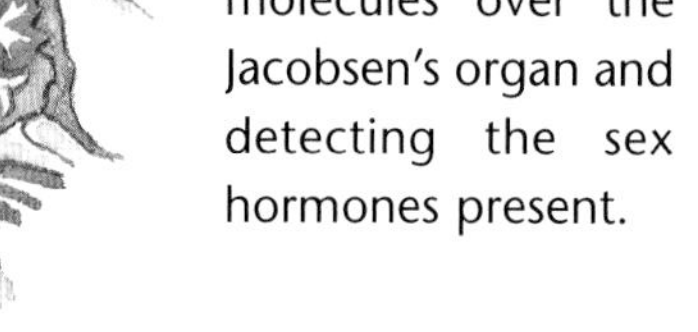

Left *The cat's senses of smell and taste are very closely linked.*

Changes in behavior show in wild and domestic cats once they are ready to mate. Overt playfulness, as displayed by this female leopard, is a sign to a male that she is nearly ready to accept his cautious advances.

BASIC INSTINCTS • Courtship

Courtship among wild felines has to be conducted with caution, since not only may there be serious conflict between rival males, but a female may at first be reluctant to accept her suitor. The relative ease with which cats can injure each other is likely to engender wariness in both partners. Lions are atypical, because they live in groups, but even in this case, the risk of the dominant males being supplanted by a rival remains high, and this can prove to be a bloody encounter.

More than one male may be attracted to a receptive female, and this often results in fighting between rival suitors. This applies to tigers also. With the high density of domestic male cats in urban areas today, combat injuries such as abscesses and torn ears are very common. Another mate-attracting technique is noise. When domestic queens (unneutered female cats) come into heat they become vocal, uttering piercing calls audible over a long distance. This enables potential mates to pinpoint her location. Some breeds, notably the Siamese and others of Oriental origin, are noisier at this stage. Once ready to mate, the female adopts a playful demeanor, becoming more affectionate. Immediately after this phase of proestrus, she will be ready to mate.

Reaching sexual maturity

The age at which a cat matures depends on the time of year they were born, their gender, and their breed. A cat that would be expected to reach maturity during the winter period of inactivity or anestrus will not mature until the following spring. Most female cats are able to breed by the time they are ten months old, but larger breeds such as the Persian longhairs are slower to mature and they may not mate successfully until they are 18 months old. At the other extreme, some Siamese queens can reach puberty when only four months old and sometimes even younger. Tom cats mature between 9 and 12 months. Like queens, they may continue to breed throughout their lives, although their fertility is likely to decline as they grow older.

A pair of tigers about to mate. In most cases, the male will subsequently take no further interest in the female, leaving her to rear the cubs on her own in due course.

Pregnancy

Since wild cats tend to lead somewhat solitary lives, there is little biological value in the females ovulating on a regular basis if there is no male available in the vicinity to mate with her. As a result, most cats have evolved a different system, which is highly unusual among mammals. This is called induced ovulation. It is the act of mating that actually triggers the release of eggs from the ovaries, thus helping to ensure that a single encounter will then result in a fertile outcome.

Practical Pointer

Do not prod your cat's abdomen to see if you can feel the fetuses in her body. This could cause injury and might even lead to their being aborted. When lifting her, take care to provide good support for her hindquarters, particularly toward the end of pregnancy, when she will be at her heaviest (see pages 118–119).

Ovulation occurs around a day after mating, at which stage spermatozoa should still be present within the female's reproductive tract; particularly as cats, certainly the larger species, will mate almost constantly in the time they remain together. In domestic cats it is often possible to tell that mating has taken place because the signs of estrus stop, before the estrus period would normally come to an end. If mating does not occur, the queen may continue to call for perhaps ten more days. There will then be a gap of about a week or so before she displays the signs of proestrus again, and the cycle continues. If mating was successful, there will be no further displays of sexual activity until after the birth of the kittens.

A successful mating

After fertilization, the ova, or eggs, will implant in the walls of the uterus, forming the placental attachment that will nourish the developing

Right *In a pride of lions, males are constantly present. They can prove to be very tolerant toward their cubs.*

kittens through pregnancy. The first external indicators of pregnancy are likely to be visible after around three weeks. At this stage, the queen's mammary glands will start to enlarge, becoming pinkish and more prominent.

Growth of the kittens themselves occurs only in the last 20 days or so of pregnancy, so as not to handicap the female unduly. This is especially important in the case of the female cheetah, who relies on her great speed to make kills and obtain food.

Fatherhood

There is a significant difference between the sexual behavior of wildcats and domestic cats. It appears that a male wildcat will mate with the same female each year, whereas tomcats are far more promiscuous. In addition, domestication has tended to dull their parenting instincts. Whereas the male wildcat hunts and obtains food for his partner while their kittens are small, this behavior is not normally seen with domestic cats, even among feral populations.

In fact, it is a good idea to keep the male separate from the female when she has young kittens. There is a risk that if she starts to come into heat soon afterward, he may attack the kittens in an urge to mate again with her.

Infanticide is also well documented among packs of lions where the dominant male in the pride has been displaced. The young cubs of lionesses are then likely to be killed by the new male. No longer having cubs to care for, these female lions will come into heat rapidly, and the newcomer then has the opportunity to make his genetic mark within the pride without delay.

BASIC INSTINCTS • Breeding potential

The reproductive potential of domestic cats tends to be higher than that of their wild relatives, particularly those from northern areas. Scottish wildcats may have up to three periods of estrus from January until May, but this does not necessarily mean that, like domestic cats, they will actually have this number of litters in a year. Observations of captive wildcats have revealed that even if they lose their kittens in the spring, they will not begin to breed again during the summer.

Although the matter is not resolved, it seems likely that true wildcats will have only a single litter in a year. Hybrids, which are more prolific (because of the input of domestic cat blood), are likely to breed more frequently. This high reproductive rate is another potential reason for hybrids appearing to have become so widespread in the wildcat population, since more of their kittens are more likely to survive and thus to breed.

Wildcats also take longer to develop, which is another factor against their producing more litters. Pregnancy in the domestic cat lasts around 60 to 63 days on average, but it is likely to take considerably longer in wildcats, extending from 63 to 69 days. In either case, a large litter is likely to result in a shorter pregnancy. The cat shown **left** is heavily pregnant and will give birth shortly.

Birth

Mother cats appreciate a quiet environment in which to give birth. In the case of a wildcat, the female will retreat to a den, the entrance to which is likely to be hidden. A kittening box may be provided for domestic cats, in a quiet part of the home, but many queens prefer to find their own place, especially if they are disturbed in the original place. Open chests of drawers are a favorite indoor spot for kittening, while a corner of a shed, surrounded by boxes, might be chosen as an alternative outdoors.

The lactation period in domestic cats lasts up to six weeks, with the weaning process beginning when the kittens are around three weeks old. They will be ready to go to a new home after 12 weeks.

The development of the wildcat is much slower. Young wildcats will not be ready to live independently until they are three and a half months old. Females tend to split away from the family group earlier than males. It is not uncommon for males to remain with the mother for up to five months. Wildcats face challenges that are not faced by their domestic relatives. They must first learn hunting skills (see page 76) and build up their strength so that they can overcome their prey once caught. These factors make it difficult for a wildcat female to produce a second litter; she must first educate her existing offspring in survival.

Newborn infants

Both wildcat and domestic kittens are born in a helpless state. It will be several days before they start moving around. The difference in weight between them is apparent from the start. It is not uncommon for some domestic kittens of the lighter breeds, such as the Siamese, to weigh little over 2oz (60g), whereas wildcat kittens will be nearly 5oz (150g) at birth. Their growth rates are roughly similar at first, with both gaining around 3oz (80g) per week.

It is vital that they suckle soon after birth, because this first milk, or colostrum, contains antibodies that will guard against infection until the kitten's own immune system becomes functional. A teat order will emerge, with the stronger kittens claiming the rear teats, which have a more nutritious output of milk.

Protecting the family

Healthy, well-fed kittens are generally quiet. This obviously has survival advantages. If an intruder approaches a wildcat litter, the mother will defend it fiercely. The domestic mother will tolerate some disturbance without reacting adversely. If you want to inspect a litter, it is a good idea to distract the female first. Repeated disturbance will cause a domestic cat to move. Each kitten will be carried by the scruff of its neck and deposited in the new site. A small litter can be moved quickly, and she may simply disappear with them, particularly if allowed out.

The eyes of kittens will be open by the time they are around ten days old, but it will be a week or so before they can start to crawl and their teeth begin to emerge. At roughly three weeks old they will be able to stand.

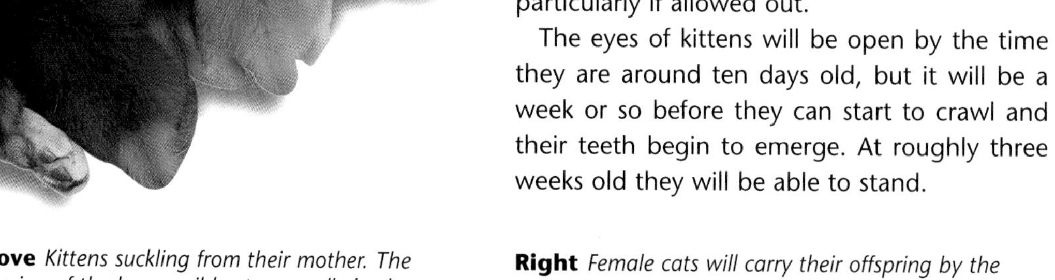

Above *Kittens suckling from their mother. The offspring of the larger wild cats are called cubs.*

Right *Female cats will carry their offspring by the scruff of the neck to a new area if they feel threatened.*

INDEPENDENCE

Growing Up

Kittens develop very rapidly but require a lot of attention from their mother, especially in the early stages. She will need to clean her offspring by licking their fur, which also stimulates them to relieve themselves. Because she needs to produce a high output of milk to support the growth of the litter, she herself will require not only plenty of food but also plenty of water to prevent dehydration.

A young Abyssinian kitten is exploring the outdoor environment. It uses its front paw rather like a hand, to investigate the area cautiously.

Both wild cubs and domestic kittens are born with blue eyes. A color change occurs in most cases — in domestic cats at around 12 weeks. (A white cat whose eyes have not changed color by this time is almost certain to be congenitally deaf; see page 32.) The color change can be quite dramatic, and not only in domestic cats. In the case of wildcats, the irises first become greenish-gray, and by five months old the color has turned a fiery yellowish-gold.

Weaning

As the kittens develop, their mother will spend longer periods of time away from them. She may even become resentful of their attempts to suckle, encouraging them instead to feed on solid food. The wildcat female will leave her litter frequently once they are beginning to eat solid food. This ensures that she can supplement their food intake by catching prey, although the male may also help in this regard.

Once young wildcats are able to move around freely, they will emerge from the den. Similarly, domestic kittens will start to range farther afield, often following their mother. It is important not to allow them to accompany her outdoors, however, as they will not have been fully vaccinated at this stage. They might also escape from the confines of your garden, squeezing through a gap in the fence or under a gate, and it could be very difficult to find them in such surroundings, especially if their mother is taking less interest in them. Listening closely for the calls of the young cat will probably provide the best way of locating it, either in the home or outdoors.

Enemies

When the mother leaves the kittens to their own devices, and if they have previously been confined on their own in a room, this can be a testing and dangerous time for them, just as it can be for wildcat kittens. This applies particularly if you have a dog, especially of the terrier type, which might show hostility toward the kittens or even kill them. Should you be in any doubt, keep the kittens in a secure pen where they will be out of the dog's reach. You can simply put the mother in with them when she starts looking around for her offspring.

BASIC INSTINCTS • Early hazards

The first few months of life can be extremely dangerous for young wild cats. They face a variety of hazards, and many will die at this stage. It has been suggested that the relatively large litters produced by those species prone to high mortality, such as the cheetah, are a natural compensation for this risk. The cheetah is especially vulnerable because of its hunting technique: it relies primarily on speed, rather than guile, to catch its quarry, and this imposes extra stresses on a growing youngster, which has yet to acquire the muscular power of a mature individual. Should it be unable to make a kill, it will become weakened, and thus be at even greater risk of dying from starvation. Cheetahs certainly rank among the most prolific of all wild cats, with females producing as many as eight offspring in a single litter, but in some areas, only one will survive up to an age of three months. Young wild cats can be killed by others of their own kind, as well as by various predators such as wild dogs.

The ferocity of the female wildcat means that these cats face virtually no predators. This is why, so long as full legal protection is given to them, their numbers should increase, enabling them to spread over a wider area, free from human persecution.

Even a fully grown red fox (*Vulpes vulpes*) will not usually seek to tackle a litter of wildcats when their mother is nearby. Her ferocity is instinctive toward any intrusion that could represent a hazard. The kittens themselves will hiss and spit menacingly if disturbed, even before their eyes are open.

On rare occasions, predatory birds can be a threat — particularly golden eagles (*Aquila chrysaetos*), but the aggression of these cats serves them well. A number of documented cases have recorded savage battles between these birds and female wildcats determined and quick enough to defend their offspring. One such battle left the wildcat so severely injured that it had to be destroyed, while the eagle was found dead nearby with horrendous injuries to its neck. However, golden eagles do often succeed in killing domestic feral cats.

It is very strange that European wildcats are instinctively so much more aggressive than their African counterparts. The explanation almost certainly relates to the greater threat to them from predators. It could be that, originally, attacks by the gray wolf (*Canis lupus*), which used to occur throughout the range of the European wildcat, but not in that of its African relative, caused this quite notable behavioral difference.

KEEPING A CAT

Choosing a Cat

The behavior of a domestic cat will be influenced by its gender, particularly if the animal is not neutered. Whereas females will call and slip out of the home in order to find a mate when they are ready to breed, mature tom cats will frequently spray urine around the home as a territorial marker.

Neutering is thus recommended, not only to prevent unwanted kittens but also to curb this type of undesirable behavior. Some owners claim that female cats are more affectionate and home-loving than males, but after neutering there is really little difference in temperament between them.

The choice between a male or female kitten is therefore normally of little significance, unless you are interested in breeding from your cat. In this case it is a good idea to start out with a female kitten. It is relatively easy to arrange for your cat to be mated with a stud tom in due course, on payment of a suitable fee.

Obviously, if you have been following the show scene by attending such events and reading the specialist press, you will be aware of the top bloodlines that are winning regularly. Your own cat, too, may have already had success on the show bench, but if you hope to improve on her features in the resulting kittens, it is important to make an honest and unprejudiced appraisal of both her strengths and her weaknesses.

If, for example, you notice that her coloration is slightly weak, it is prudent to seek out a sire with very strong coloring. In this way, some of the kittens may show an improvement in their coloration over that of their mother.

Although there can be no guarantees, this approach is most likely to lead to an overall improvement in the quality of your cats.

Choosing can be difficult when confronted with a litter of attractive kittens, such as these Somalis. They are six weeks old, and not yet fully weaned.

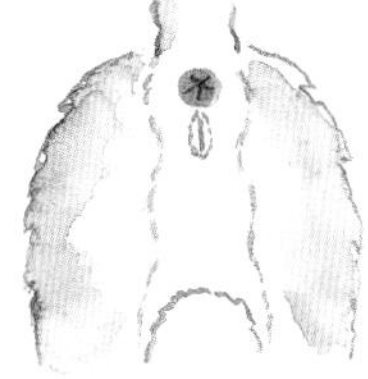
Female kitten. Note proximity of ano-genital openings.

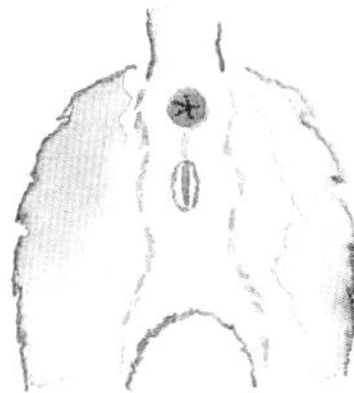
Female cat. Similar in appearance, but a slightly larger space is evident.

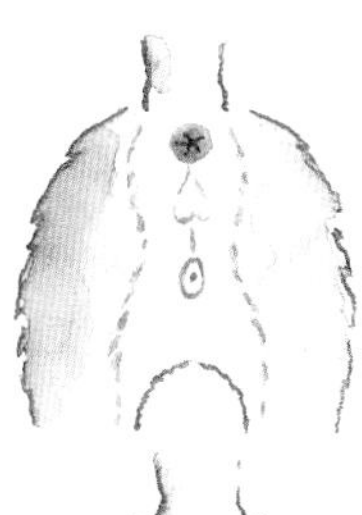
Male kitten. Larger gap than in the female, although testes have not descended.

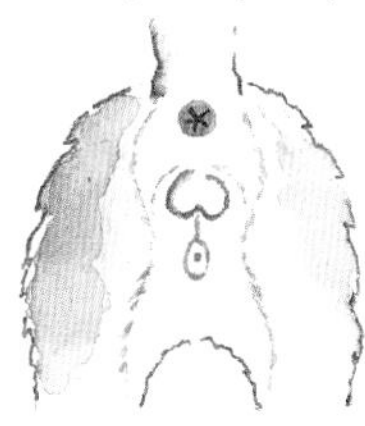
Male cat. Testes clearly visible in the scrotum by this stage.

Sexing

Sexing kittens is certainly not as easy as it is for adult cats, because their genitals tend to be less pronounced. It is helpful to compare the kittens in a litter if you are in any doubt. Determining their sex becomes fairly straightforward once the young cats are roughly a month old.

A male cat does not have an external penis. Like the female, he has two visible openings below the base of the tail, the upper opening being the anus, but the gap between them is longer than in a female. The penile orifice also tends to be more rounded in shape, whereas the vulval opening in the female resembles a slit. Should you still be in doubt, gentle pressure on each side of the opening in the male should bring the penis into view. A cat's penis is unusual, being covered in tiny spines that stick up during mating.

The testes will become evident in male kittens at around four weeks of as swellings between the anus and the penile opening. Before this stage, the testes will have descended from the abdomen, where they develop, but will not project into the scrotum.

As a cat matures, it becomes easier, particularly in some breeds, to determine its sex simply by looking at it. Male British shorthairs, for example, develop very distinct swellings on either side of the face, known as jowls, which are not apparent in females. As in the case of many wildcats, they also tend to be slightly larger than females.

BASIC INSTINCTS • Manes

The most recognizable sexual characteristic in wild cats is the mane of the male lion. Various factors have influenced the growth of the mane. Lions from colder areas have more highly developed manes than those in warm climates, and the feature also varies between subspecies. In the case of the distinctive Barbary race of the lion (*Panthera l. leo*), which used to be found in North Africa, the mane was black and extended down the back and along the underparts.

Male lions do not start to grow a mane until they are around three years old, and at this stage it is pale in color. The development of the lion's mane is under the control of the male sex hormones; neutering a male lion, even after puberty, will cause the mane to recede and ultimately disappear.

Practical Pointer

It is a mistaken belief that all tortoiseshell cats are female. Although they are very likely to be female, there is a rare genetic quirk that can produce a tortoiseshell appearance in a male. Such tortoiseshells have an additional chromosome and are usually sterile, but otherwise these cats are normal.

Taking a kitten home

Choosing a healthy kitten is reasonably straightforward, provided that you follow a few basic guidelines. Start by looking at the kitten's head, checking that its ears are clean, its eyes are bright, and that there is no discharge from the nose or repeated sneezing. Check the coat for signs of fleas, and make sure that the kitten can move easily, without any evidence of stiffness. Lift the tail to ensure there is no soiling here, which could indicate diarrhea. If you are in doubt about a kitten, it is probably best not to pursue your interest in it. Otherwise you could be leaving yourself open to high veterinary costs and undue worry over your new pet's health right from the outset.

While most people instinctively favor a kitten when selecting a cat, there are many older cats that need good homes for a variety of reasons. If you are considering an adult cat, try to find out as much as possible about its background before making a final decision. It can obviously be harder to integrate a stray cat into the home, compared with a home-loving cat whose previous owner may have died.

However, adult cats can settle satisfactorily in the home, provided that they are kept indoors for at least two weeks and ideally up to a month, before being let out. These cats may prove to be nervous, however, if they have been living as strays, and their toilet training may be more problematical.

Below *Domestic kittens such as this cream Burmese have highly playful natures, and will soon adapt to new surroundings.*

When choosing a kitten from a litter you should ensure it is fairly lively and has a natural curiosity. This is a good sign that you have chosen a responsive pet. You should also look out for the points mentioned below.

Any faint tabby marking are likely to fade as the cat grows older. In the case of longhairs, their coats are less profuse at this age compared with adults.

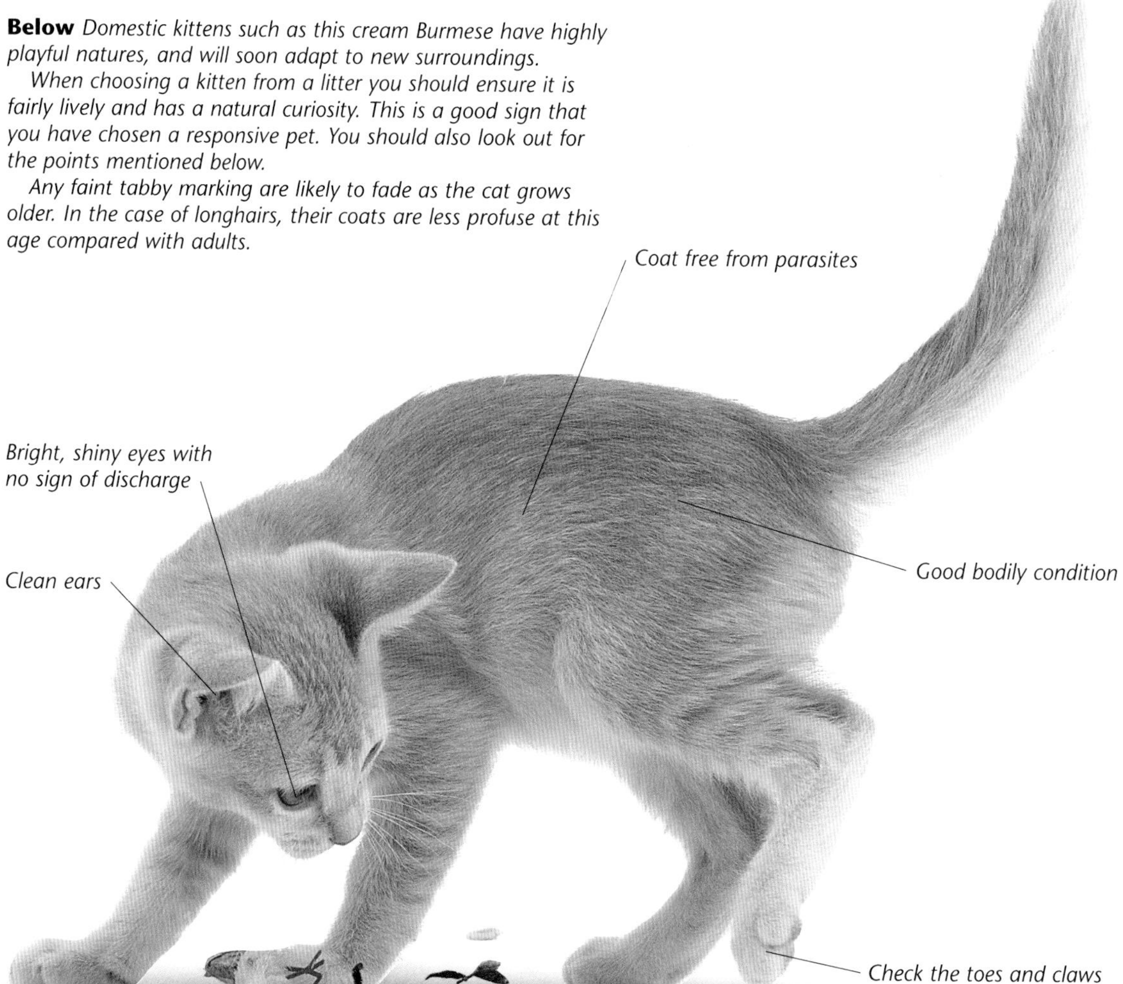

Cats and dogs

On balance, a kitten is likely to be a better choice, particularly if you already have a dog. Ultimately, the cat will probably prove dominant to its canine companion. While a kitten will simply turn and hiss and may paw at the dog if it persists in its attentions, an older cat is likely to act more decisively. Like its wildcat ancestor, the domestic cat will seek to escape by leaping off the ground onto a higher level — in this case furniture — and will remain here scowling at the dog. While cats are usually careful, they can knock over and break things under these circumstances, so try to supervise encounters in the early stage. Should it be cornered, the cat is likely to scratch the dog. This can be sufficient to deter the most determined dog, and the resulting wounds may need veterinary attention.

Practical Pointer

Never leave your cat alone in a vehicle, even for a short time, especially during the summer. The temperature in a locked car can rise within a few minutes to a fatal level.

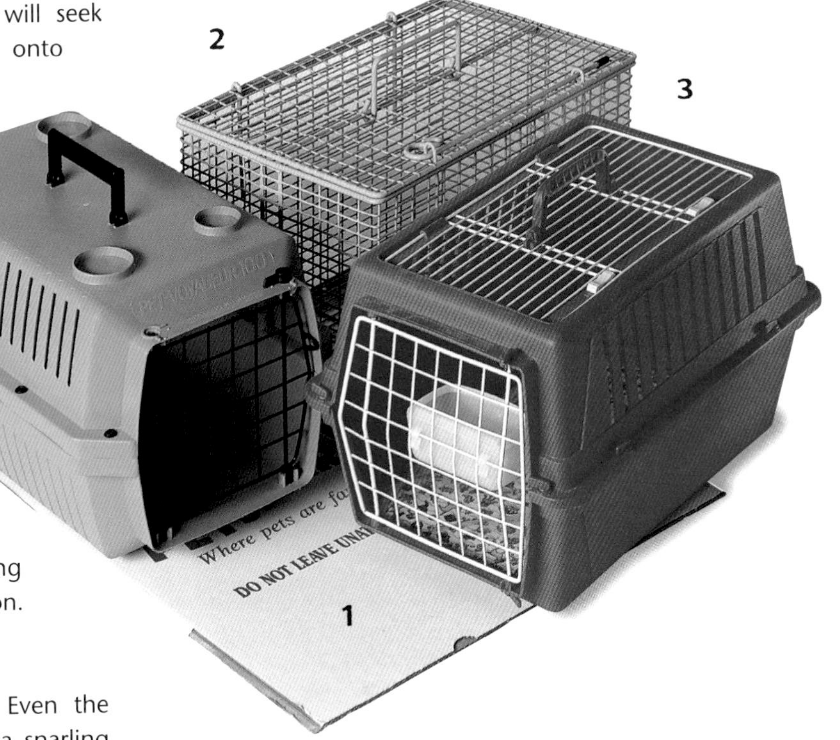

A selection of modern cat carriers are shown here. They can all be easily cleaned. Check the door fastening, and the ease with which the cat can be moved in and out of the carrier. Cats often revert to the aggressive ways of their wildcat ancestor when traveling if they are unused to the experience.

Cat carriers

Transporting cats can be difficult. Even the most passive pussycat can become a snarling terror on a car journey, so do not be tempted to take your pet out unless it is in a secure carrier. There are various designs on the market. Cardboard carriers **1** are the cheapest option, but they are not very durable nor are they particularly secure. If you do need to carry a cat in a cardboard box, be sure to tape both the bottom and top securely and provide ventilation holes around the side.

Open mesh carriers such as baskets **2** are secure, but cats rarely settle well in them. They will constantly seek to escape, and will meow loudly. Urine will also seep out, if the cat relieves itself, and the odor can permeate a car's upholstery for a long time afterward.

Basket-type carriers also have their hazards. A cat may catch its claw in the wickerwork, if not supervised; and if a strand comes loose it might injure the cat's eye. Moreover, these carriers are virtually impossible to clean.

A part-mesh plastic carrier **3** or a hooded plastic carrier with a mesh front **4** gives the cat more security, so it should feel more settled here, especially if it is lined with a blanket. Cleanliness is not a problem, and if the top half of the carrier can be detached, it should be easy to remove even a recalcitrant cat safely.

Cats can be taught to use a cat flap without too much difficulty. The reason may be linked with the way that their wild ancestors will venture through small openings into dens.

Settling in

When it arrives in a new home, a cat will start to explore its new surroundings, cautiously at first, pausing to sniff at intervals, like a wildcat, while remaining alert to sounds in its vicinity. Kittens will settle in a new environment much more readily than older cats. This reflects their behavior in the wild; after weaning, wildcat kittens will normally wander away from the area where they were reared, in search of a territory of their own.

Whereas wildcats will fiercely resist attempts to pick them up, domestic kittens will respond very favorably to handling from the time that they are starting to move around on their own. If they are not exposed to human company at this stage, however, kittens are likely to remain shy in character, just like feral kittens which are reared in isolation from people, often in underground burrows.

Although the female cats carry their kittens by the scruff of the neck when they are young, this is not the way to carry them yourself. Pick the kitten up by placing your hand under its belly and tuck it into your body, so that the young cat feels secure. With its underparts adequately supported, it will be far less likely to struggle or scratch. Making a fuss over the kitten and calling it to come when you are providing food will also help to establish a bond between you.

Young kittens will often hide away at times in the home, seeking cover just like their wild relatives in a territory. Before long, you will come to recognize their routine — it may be under a table or chest where they prefer to sleep, rather than in the bed that you have provided for them. This can indicate that the bed itself may be located in an area of the home where the young cat feels insecure. Moving the bed to the cat's favorite sleeping area may see it used more often.

Off limits

If there are areas of the home where you do not want the kitten to venture, keep these closed off from the outset. If, for example, it becomes used to sleeping in your bedroom over the first six months, you will find it much harder to ban the cat from the bedroom subsequently.

It is actually not a good idea to allow the cat to share your bed, because this is the easiest way to be bitten by fleas! Also, such close contact may make you allergic to your pet.

Practical Pointer

Even domestic cats still retain quite strong nocturnal tendencies, which means that they will sleep for long periods during the day. This is quite normal, with kittens sleeping for 16 hours each day or even longer.

Above *The curiosity of cats means that they will investigate items around the home, being attracted here to play with the fringe on a chair. They may even resort to chewing such items.*

Practical Pointer

Kittens like to seek out a snug, warm spot to sleep, just like their wildcat ancestors. In the home they can be tempted to slip into a clothes dryer or a washing machine, with potentially catastrophic consequences. Always check inside such machines before running them, because a kitten may have slipped inside unseen.

Although work is proceeding on a vaccine against this allergy, it still afflicts many people, and its effects can be devastating, even forcing you to seek another home for your cat. The signs are runny eyes and nose and a tight-chested feeling — making it difficult to breathe. Asthmatics are probably at greatest risk of developing an allergy. Longhaired breeds are most likely to have this effect, but any cat can cause symptoms in a rather sensitized individual.

One room that may hold specific dangers for the cat is the bathroom or lavatory. Although cats are widely believed to dislike water (see pages 124 –125), it is not unusual for them to seek to drink from the toilet bowl, and they may even bathe in here. Should you have the cat's litter box located here, do be sure to keep the toilet lid closed at all times — this is often something that needs to be impressed on children.

Below *Cats are always on the look-out for secure localities for sleeping. A cat will often hop into a cardboard box and then curl up inside.*

Safety for your cat

You should allow a kitten to go outside only after it has completed its vaccinations. This can be done after around 12 weeks. This confinement to quarters gives your pet time to become established in the home and, hopefully, to respond to its name. Once the young cat is allowed to roam farther afield, you need to be able to persuade it to come back to you when necessary. Food is useful for this purpose, so start by letting your kitten play in the garden and then calling it back to be fed.

Danger on wheels

There is a real risk today, especially in urban surroundings, that your cat could be badly hurt or killed by traffic. This is most likely to occur during the evening. The dark markings of many cats help to conceal their presence, and although such camouflage may help wildcats, it can be catastrophic for domestic cousins.

The driver does not see the cat, which may have run out from behind a parked vehicle, until it is really too late to brake safely. The cat, instead of using its speed to escape, turns and is dazzled by the headlights. In this situation, its reflexes are of little value, and it will almost certainly be hit.

In daylight, however, both driver and cat have a greater chance of avoiding a collison. Unfortunately, cats do not develop any road sense, even after being injured in this way.

Car accidents are now one of the major causes of premature death among young pet cats in many urban areas.

Practical Pointer

Consider fitting your cat with a safe elasticized collar, attaching a disk or capsule to it that gives your phone number and address. Then if it does stray elsewhere, or becomes involved in an accident, you can be informed. There is nothing worse than having a pet simply disappear.

Safety measures

It is possible to avoid this risk by keeping your cat indoors permanently, providing a well equipped play area in the home instead. Alternatively, you can often train kittens to walk on special harnesses similar to those sold for small dogs, with a leash attached. This does restrict your cat's ability to exercise, however, and clearly it is not a good idea to allow it out onto the street, in case you meet a dog which frightens your pet. It will then roll around, trying to break free from the harness, and is likely to bite or scratch you, should you then try to pick it up.

A much safer compromise will be to construct an outside run for the cat in your garden. Here it will be able to exercise during the day and can then be brought in at night. Even so, there should be a snug shelter attached to the run, where the cat can sleep for periods during the day. There are specialist firms advertising in the cat magazines that make runs of this type,

Play and climbing frames like this are very popular with cats, providing hours of activity for them. Be sure to offer equipment of this type to cats that are kept permanently indoors.

although you could construct one quite easily yourself, building the mesh panels to fit around a garden shed, which will act as the shelter.

Slabs should be used to create a floor covering which can be disinfected easily; and a secure door is essential, to deter vandals. Branches and other climbing facilities provided in the run must be firmly supported, and there must be no loose sharp ends of mesh accessible to the cat, as they could cause injury.

Practical Pointer

There are a number of poisons that cats may come into contact with outdoors, ranging from slug pellets to rodenticides. One of the deadliest is anti-freeze, used in cars. Cats apparently like its taste and drink it readily. This will lead to rapid death from kidney failure, so be sure to keep it, and other poisons, well away from your cat.

Always try to keep a watch on a young kitten when it is allowed out for the first time, because it could end up in danger.

CATS TOGETHER

Catteries of this type are available in sectional form. They provide plenty of space for exercise, and are used by breeders for show stock. A snug shelter provides protection in bad weather.

Cats are not social by nature, reflecting the independent traits of their wildcat ancestor, but as domestication advances, so they have become tolerant of each other. Immediate family members, such as a mother cat and her older kittens will remain friendly.

Catteries

Cats are sensitive creatures and soon detect the change in routine leading up to a house move, or your departure on vacation. They may disappear, which can make for great difficulties if you want to take your pet to a cattery and then go straight on to the airport. It is always advisable to take your pet to the cattery on the day before your departure. Putting the cat into a cattery during a move is also recommended.

The best way to locate a good cattery in your area is to ask friends and relatives or your veterinarian for advice. Or, you can phone several and arrange to visit them before you leave. This will give you the opportunity to compare the facilities and the personnel before making a final decision. Satisfied customers will return repeatedly to a cattery, and often there is no space during holidays. Reserve a place early.

Good facilities

The cats should be housed individually, unless they are used to being together, or their natural territorial instincts can lead to bullying and fighting. There should be an outside run and indoor heating available if the weather is cold.

The surroundings should be clean, and secure, with a double door entrance system of some kind so that a cat cannot get out. Although it might return to its own neighborhood, there is no guarantee of this, and being scared and in strange surroundings, the cat is likely to remain hidden for some time.

Not all cats settle well. Some refuse food so tell them what your cat normally eats. A cat that has never been in these surroundings before is more likely to lose its appetite than one that has often stayed. If your cat settles easily, this is a good sign for the future.

Part of the difficulty is the cat's natural shyness. If it is disturbed at a kill, a wildcat will retreat, taking its food if possible. It will not eat in the open. A domestic cat in the confines of a cattery is most likely to sample its food at night, if this is placed in a quiet corner where there is some cover, such as under a climbing frame.

The cattery's requirements

All reputable catteries will insist on seeing your cat's vaccination certificate. With cats under a higher degree of stress than would be the case at home, and when a number share the same air space indoors in a cattery block, the likelihood of an outbreak of disease is higher. Catteries often request payment in advance, especially from customers whom they do not know, because owners sometimes dump unwanted pets, give a false name and address, and never return. Always leave the cattery a means of contacting you in an emergency. At the very least, give them the name and telephone number of your veterinarian.

New friends — or not?

If you already have a cat, introducing another one to the home may prove problematic. Some cats are more amenable than others to sharing a home with another of their own kind. It is not possible to tell how things will progress until the cats are together, although introducing them carefully may help to prevent problems.

If you think you will want two cats, it is best to obtain two kittens together from the same litter. They will grow up with little friction between them, and they are likely to remain affectionate toward each other. Of course, one of the two will dominate the other, but this is established almost from the moment of birth. Once this is established, the risk of conflict is reduced. Bringing together older cats that do not know each other is more difficult, although a kitten and an older female will usually get along well without problems, particularly if the kitten itself is also female.

Two cats that know each other well will often wash each other to reinforce the bond between them.

Cat protocol

If you already have an adult cat, it is best to choose a kitten for its companion, because the social dominance will be established by their respective ages, whereas with two older cats this will take longer. Bring the young cat to the older cat, but do not place it next to your established pet. Allow them to get acquainted at their own pace. You should remain in the vicinity in case fighting does occur, in which case you will need to separate the cats.

Conflict often occurs over food, so try to feed the cats separately — although your established cat may steal some food from the newcomer if the latter eats slowly. It is better not to interfere because it means that your new cat is accepting a subordinate role. Provide more food once the other cat has finished eating, so the newcomer will not be hungry.

In the early stages it can be difficult to allow one cat to roam while keeping the other confined, if you have a cat flap, but it is essential to prevent straying.

Toilet troubles

Be prepared for a breakdown in the toilet training of the established cat. It is a difficult problem and is most likely to arise when the established cat is a male. In time, once the scent of the newcomer pervades the home, the other cat will accept that they are sharing this territory and desist from this behavior. The cats will get used to each other but they should never be forced together and must always be transported separately. At worst they will display a sullen mutual contempt, and avoid each other at home. However, there is every possibility that a bond will develop to the extent that they will groom each other and play together. Even so, they are unlikely to become inseparable companions if they have been introduced later in life.

Communica

TION & BEHAVIOR

Cats are not always well disposed toward each other, being strongly territorial by nature; and although domestic cats have devised means of lessening the risk of disputes arising, by sharing territories, fights — and resulting injuries — are by no means uncommon. Neutering will help to reduce the likelihood of your cat being badly injured in a fight, but this provides no absolute guarantee. Outbreaks of aggression are unfortunately very hard to prevent in the case of cats that roam free. Equally, it can be difficult to discourage other instinctive feline behavior patterns, such as hunting, although there are ways in which you can help to protect the local wildlife population from your cat. And although domestic cats are far less responsive to training than dogs, you may be able to teach your cat to obey some basic commands if you start when it is very young.

COMMUNICATION

The Cat's Language

Cats communicate in many ways — not just vocally but also, and very revealingly, through body language. The way in which they lie, any movements of their tail, and the position of their ears all reflect their mood. Even their eyelids can be significant in this respect. A cat with half-closed eyes is invariably relaxed and resting.

A kitten is completely helpless at first, and is totally dependent on its mother. Its mother's purrs may provide reassurance.

Purring

Purring is a sign of contentment in cats, although it is unclear how they produce this sound. From kittenhood onward, cats will purr. The conventional explanation is that this sound is made by changes in air pressure around the voice box, or larynx, resulting from the vibration of the false vocal cords — a distinctive feature of the cat's anatomy situated just in front of the larynx itself (see page 44). In some cases a cat may be purring without making a sound, but the vibration can be detected by placing a finger gently on its throat.

Another explanation that is now given less credence relates to the flow of blood through the *posterior vena cava*, which is the major vein that returns blood to the heart from the abdominal area and hind limbs. Changes in the flow rate may cause turbulence, setting up a vibration in the sinuses of the head, transmitted here along the windpipe.

The purring reflex is generally a sign of contentment. It is thought to have arisen as a way for kittens to communicate with their mother. Evidence supporting this theory is the fact that purring can take place while the kitten is suckling. It is also a very quiet sound, which is not audible from a long distance away, and thus its communication potential is limited to someone who is very close by — such as a nursing mother.

Purring seems to be a common trait among all the smaller wild felines. Wildcat kittens will also purr, and in them, as in domestic kittens, this ability develops from the age of around a week. Adult female wildcats will themselves purr when they are relaxed, with their kittens, although they purr less frequently than their domestic counterparts.

Greetings

Members of a pair, in the case of both wild cats and domestic cats, that know each other well, will greet each other by direct contact, with one individual rubbing its head on the cheeks of the other. This action serves to transfer scent. Although this type of communication has not been well studied in the case of many wildcats, it does appear to be far more prevalent in some species, such as Pallas's cat, than in others, although

BASIC INSTINCTS • Vocalization

Vocal communication in wild cats is most pronounced in the case of larger species, such as in this snow leopard shown below, which do not need to conceal their presence from predators — apart from humans. The smaller wildcats are much more secretive, and will not often reveal their position by calling. They will, however, use vocalizations to intimidate a potential rival, both before a fight and during it, when they may utter very piercing sounds.

Female domestic cats will often seek to defend their young in a similar way, shrieking to intimidate a would-be attacker.

Practical Pointer

Cats will react to your tone of voice. Speaking quietly can help to calm a nervous cat, especially if you can stroke it at the same time, but take care that it does not scratch you.

in this case these cats tend to rub their bodies rather than just their heads.

In the case of the small wildcats, belonging to the *Felis* genus, their vocal prowess is considerably weaker compared to that of their larger relatives such as lions. This relates to the structure of the hyoid apparatus, which is located in the vicinity of the throat.

In small cats, the larynx is attached to the skull by the hyoid (Y-shaped) bones (see page 22. Among the members of the *Panthera* genus (large cats), the arrangement is different: Cartilage replaces the bone. This gives greater flexibility, and, along with their much larger chest cavity, allows them to roar loudly, with their calls carrying over a great distance.

When an adult cat is relaxed it will often stretch out in this way on its back, purring loudly with its mouth usually closed.

Body language

The European wildcat's reputation for aggression has led to stories about how a cornered animal will leap at a person's throat. Generally, however, like other wild cats, it relies for survival more on its ability to escape detection than on its fighting prowess. If it is challenged, it can put up a fierce fight, being significantly stronger than a domestic cat, but in fact, a wildcat will rely on body language initially to avoid any combat.

Aggression

The wildcat's gestures are actually somewhat different from those seen in a domestic cat under threat. When facing perceived danger, a domestic cat will adopt a side-on stance, also raising its fur to enhance its size, whereas a wild cat will try to stare down its opponent with its yellow eyes burning fiercely, standing upright.

Above *This cat is curious but slightly unsure. Note the way in which its head is stretched forward and its tail is held in a relatively horizontal position.*

The wildcat assumes a more head-on position than its domestic relative, being comparatively larger to begin with. Slowly and carefully, it will back toward any available support behind it, such as rocks or a tree stump, presumably to lessen the risk of being attacked from behind.

A domestic cat which is challenging another aggressively will raise its ears and constrict its pupils, while lashing its tail up and down. Vocalization is also significant: First comes a warning hiss, followed by snarling and wailing, which give way to ferocious spitting sounds if the combatants start to clash.

Dealing with a cat in shock

When cats become distressed, they can become aggressive even toward their owners; this is particularly true if the cat has been involved in a road accident. It will be suffering from shock, even if it is not apparently severely injured, and you will need to take the cat to your veterinarian for a checkup. The signs of

Left *Cats can build up a strong bond with people they know well, allowing themselves to be picked up and carried. Such behavior is not seen in wild cats.*

potentially life-threatening problems, such as internal hemorrhaging, may not be immediately evident to you at this stage.

You are likely to need to handle your cat and transport it in a carrier (see page 55). Even a tame cat may bite or scratch in this type of situation, and a feral cat can be exceedingly aggressive; so protect yourself to minimize the risk of being injured. Thick garden gloves will help, although they may not be strong enough to withstand a cat's canines. It is also essential to wear a well-padded coat and tuck the sleeves in the gloves. Otherwise there might be a gap, leaving your wrist painfully exposed. Place the carrier as near to the cat as possible, with the lid or door open so that it will be relatively easy to place the cat straight in here, once you have restrained it.

Try to take hold of the cat's neck first, effectively pressing it down toward the ground so that it will have difficulty swiveling around and using its claws; also, it will not be able to turn its head easily from this position. Then use the loose skin on the scruff of the neck to lift the cat straight into its carrier, closing the lid immediately afterward. You will probably require someone to help you in order to execute this tricky operation successfully.

Practical Pointer

Teach children to handle the family cat gently, and discourage them from trying to lift it unless you are present to supervise. Otherwise they are likely to be scratched or even bitten.

BASIC INSTINCTS • The value of ears

The lithe body of the cat enables it to adopt a wide variety of postures, which serve to indicate its mood and intentions. This so-called body language is very similar throughout the cat family. You can tell immediately that this Scottish wildcat is in an aggressive posture.

The ears of cats are especially important in this respect. If threatening a rival, a wildcat brings its ears forward to make itself look more imposing. A weaker individual will then respond to this challenge by flattening its ears in a submissive gesture and retreating.

Practical Pointer

Some cats have a worrying and very painful trait of apparently being quite relaxed with their owners and then suddenly striking an aggressive posture, lashing out unexpectedly with their claws. It is hard to stop this behavior, but avoiding stroking the cat's underparts usually prevents this problem.

FIRST ENCOUNTERS

How Cats Settle Disputes

When cats first encounter each other, it is not easy for the casual observer to tell from their behavior which is the aggressive and which the submissive one. However, there are clear indications that the cats understand perfectly.

Exposing its teeth in this way is a typical sign of aggression in a cat, when accompanied by hissing.

Submission

Most wild cats rarely come into contact with each other, living solitary lives and ranging over territories that may be typically 170 acres (70 hectares) in area. But domestic cats live in close proximity to each other, and among them disputes are more common.

Usually one cat will approach the other closely, sniffing in the region of its tail, and thus taking the dominant role. The other cat will generally respond in a submissive way, by lowering its ears flat against the head, rather than holding them vertically. Its pupils will dilate, so that they appear to be more prominent. It will also keep its tail tucked down.

If the other cat continues to circle, the submissive individual may hesitate briefly then decide to look for an escape route and run off. This action may be sufficient to deter any real outbreak of aggression by the other cat. The cat that issued the challenge has made its point emphatically, and with its dominance unquestioned it moves off elsewhere.

Some domestic cats appear to be more aggressive than others. This is often related to their gender, with intact males frequently engaging in territorial disputes with others in the area. The legacy of fights — in the form of infected wounds which frequently need veterinary treatment — can be crippling for the cat and expensive for the owner, but there is

Practical Pointer

The weather can affect your cat's mood, and may cause it to be aggressive, particularly if it becomes frightened. Thunder and lightning can be very disturbing to cats, which seem able to sense the oncoming change in the weather. If they are outdoors, they may also disappear for a time after a bad storm. Fireworks can have a similar effect.

very little that can be done to prevent such conflicts other than neutering your male and keeping him indoors, especially at night.

Dealing with hostility

A worse situation can arise in the home, where a cat may learn to turn submission into aggression. Rough handling by children will make the cat reluctant to come within reach. If cornered, it may decide to swipe at the child with its claws. The child will then run off in pain, or at least will be reluctant to disturb the cat at that time. If this sequence is repeated, the cat will soon realize that by behaving in this way it will be left alone.

Scolding the cat is unlikely to have any effect. Cats do not respond to punishment of any kind by mending their ways. The only solution is to let time take its course. Eventually the cat will learn to accept the child, while remaining well-disposed throughout toward other members of the family.

Feline invaders

Some cats can be so territorial by inclination that — not content with being aggressive toward their neighbors outdoors — they will actually pursue them into their homes, if a cat flap is available. In these more confined surroundings, fighting is even more likely to break out than in the garden. You are also likely to be confronted with the lingering smell of cat urine sprayed indoors, either by your cat or by a rival determined to stake a claim to this territory. This often occurs unexpectedly at night, so that you may be woken up with the sounds of cats confronting each other indoors.

Under these circumstances, the only way to prevent a likely repetition is to dispense with the cat flap, encouraging your cat to stay in of its own accord at night. This can be achieved more easily by feeding your pet in the evening as a routine, so that it will be hungry and come inside seeking food. Alternatively, you will need a cat flap that only your cat can open, by wearing a special elasticized collar that is equipped with a magnet.

Practical Pointer

Young cats may start to become very aggressive when they are playing. The best thing to do is to intervene and to stop the game at this point. Hopefully, this will cause them to stop such behavior in the future.

The cat on the right is clearly upset by the presence of the other cat. It is responding very aggressively while the cat on the left has decided to withdraw, rather than stand its ground.

BEHAVIOR

Out of all the behavioral traits of cats, aggression and the ability to get into fights with other animals is one of the most worrying to owners. Cats are still highly territorial creatures by nature, and the risk of aggressive encounters is increased in urban areas where cats live at high densities.

Fighting

Cats have the ability to inflict some severe and painful injuries with their teeth and claws, thanks to their agile bodies and quick reflexes. But having elicited a painful response of this type, the cat will usually seek to escape, running off rapidly as was its intention before it was cornered and restrained.

In a neighborhood where there are domestic cats, the situation is changing regularly, with people moving in and out of the area, along with their pets. As a result, the territorial situation is not static. In fact, the introduction of a new cat can cause some serious upsets, particularly if it is an intact tom cat.

When fighting breaks out, it usually proves to be a fierce but brief encounter. The weaker individual soon breaks off, darting away when it can.

Almost certainly, the newcomer and the established tom cat will clash, sometimes repeatedly. Where there are two cats intent on occupying a territory, serious fighting can occur. Having exhausted all the preliminary hostile gestures, neither giving way, the two combatants square up to each other in earnest.

The cat that was originally challenged seeks to assert itself, switching from a submissive attitude to displaying a more aggressive manner, starting by curling its tail into a U-shape. It displays its body side-on, to emphasize its strength, while all the time keeping its ears pressed down against the head. This individual will also be snarling loudly at this stage, with its mouth wide open.

Total war

When the aggressor strikes, the other cat will roll over with all its claws exposed, so that it can use the power of its feet to maximum effect. Both cats will now be spitting firecely, and

Practical Pointer

If you encounter cats fighting, do not try to break them up by interfering directly, as you will inevitably be scratched or bitten. Instead, throw a bowl of water over them, which should separate them almost immediately. They are likely to fight again, though, at some point in the future.

Pumas fighting. A cat on its back is clearly very vulnerable to its opponent, although even in the wild cats rarely kill each other. However, nasty infections can develop from their bites.

direct contact is likely to lead to injury, typically in the vicinity of the head and neck, although it could be virtually anywhere on the body.

The actual period of contact is likely to be quite brief, partly because of the ferocity of the combat. The weaker individual will break free and run off fast, pursued by the victor for some distance. Fighting is most likely to occur during the breeding season, and some cats will clash repeatedly during this period. It is not unknown for the subordinate individual to be driven away by the constant battling against a rival.

The worst situation arises when the cats are evenly matched, and a young male cat seeks to displace an older, established male. Repeated fighting will occur until the situation is resolved. Cats will not battle to the death, even though they might be capable of killing each other.

BASIC INSTINCTS • Leader of the pride

In wild cats, fighting tends to be most prevalent among lions, where males will battle for supremacy to lead a pride. Young males live solitary lives, being driven out as youngsters and living largely on their own until they are old and strong enough to drive out an established male. The period of supremacy is often brief, lasting just a year or so, but it has the effect of ensuring that new genes are introduced into the pride at regular intervals.

TERRITORIES

How Cats Claim an Area

Above *Scratching against tree trunks helps to sharpen the cat's claws, but also serves as a territorial marker.*

There are several subtle ways in which domestic cats claim areas of territory, even when they are not present in the garden. This is achieved, just as in the wild, by a combination of olfactory and visual indicators that will be detected by other cats in the neighborhood. Each cat will then have to decide whether it wishes to provoke a possible confrontation by crossing these borders.

Cats will often have a favorite scratching post in the yard or garden — perhaps a tree or a fence post. The site chosen is usually in a prominent position, and it will be visited on a regular basis. When scratching here, the cat may appear rather angry, keeping its ears flattened.

This behavior has two purposes. Firstly, it serves to keep the cat's claws sharp, which is important because walking and climbing regularly wears down the tips, even though they are kept retracted. More importantly, though, in a territorial sense, the distinct pattern of scratching in a prominent spot will reveal to another cat that this territory is already occupied and warn it to keep away.

Scents and sensitivity

The cat will also have left its scent when scratching. Between the toes are sweat glands for this purpose. Regular scratching will serve to reinforce the scent here, rather than allowing it to fade. For cats living in the home therefore, a scratching post will be an important item, allowing them to mimic their natural behavior indoors. It also lessens the possibility that they will use a piece of furniture for this purpose.

Cats also spray their urine as a further way of scent marking, and this is sufficiently pungent, particularly in the case of tom cats, to be easily detected by our noses. The smell is highly unpleasant and lingers for a long time; it is also sufficiently individual for other cats to be able to recognize it. Male cats spray more frequently than females, being more territorial by nature. The location of the cat's penis — on its bottom, rather than on the underside of the body (as in dogs, for example) — assists with scent marking. Because it sprays backward, the tom cat can target sites, such as gates and fences, where other cats are likely to pass, and at a height where the scent can be easily detected.

The frequency of spraying outdoors is determined by a number of factors. If there is a strange cat in the area, the frequency will increase. Similarly, heavy rain, which will ultimately wash away the scent, will trigger more spraying, possibly in a drier place, such as a front door protected by a porch.

Practical Pointer

The only effective way to stop a cat from using a particular tree for scratching purposes is to encircle the base with plastic or wire mesh.

Lynxes are found in parts of Europe and North America. Cats occur in a wide variety of terrain from dense tropical forests to treeless areas with bitterly cold winters.

Above *Cats will establish distinct territories, with tom cats ranging over the widest area. In some cases, territories will be shared between individuals, and there may be invisible pathways (white area in illustration) which cats will use to cross the territory of a neighbor without the risk of any conflict arising.*

Wildcats' boundaries

Wildcats of different species display very similar behavior. In the case of servals, for example, males may spray urine up to 46 times per hour — over twice as often as females. While domestic cats are somewhat less territorial than their wild relatives, living at much higher densities than wildcats, the need to establish boundaries is still strong. In some instances, they may even use their feces for this purpose, depositing them in a prominent position rather than burying them, as is usual. Such behavior is especially likely following the introduction of a new cat to the household, so that two cats must now share an identical range. The feces themselves pick up the individual scent of the cat, from glands just inside the anus.

The marking of territorial borders in this fashion is particularly common in the big cats, such as tigers, but rarer in the *Felis* species. This may be because of the greater need of

Right *It may appear as a simple gesture of affection, but when a cat rubs against your legs or on a chair it is really scent-marking, leaving a sign of its territory.*

BASIC INSTINCTS • Size of territory

The size of a wildcat's territory is influenced by a number of factors, among the most significant being the availability of prey.

Bigger wild cats, such as tigers, may have larger territories, simply because their prey is likely to be at lower density than the rodents and birds which form the bulk of the diet of the wildcat itself. With the increasing pressure of human settlement (quite apart from hunting), it is difficult to provide tigers with the space needed to maintain viable populations. Development often slices up their territories, pushing the remaining wild cats in isolated pockets. This has happened in the case of the Florida puma (*Felis concolor coryi*); even the construction of special tunnels under roads has not prevented some of these highly endangered cats from being killed by traffic.

When cats, and especially big cats in the wild, have won a territiory and feel relatively secure they can spend time relaxing. As shown by this cheetah, they may stretch out and roll over onto their backs.

small cats to conceal their presence from other carnivores, including their own larger relatives. The territorial marking by smaller cats is more subtle. Outdoors, they may rub their heads on certain branches; indoors, they may like to rub the side of their mouth on a corner of the wall. In both cases the aim is to deposit scent from their sebaceous glands at this spot.

Practical Pointer

A cat may be reluctant to use a scratching post at first, so gently raise its front paws and slide them down the post. Repeat this several times, and the cat should then return here of its own accord.

HUNTING

It was the hunting skills of the wildcat, demonstrated to our distant agrarian ancestors, that led ultimately to the cat's domestication. Even today, domestic cats often prove to be avid hunters; they kill millions of birds and small animals. Trying to discourage cats from behaving in this way can be difficult. However, some breeds, such as Persian longhairs, tend to have less developed hunting instincts than others such as Siamese.

Above *Cats hunt instinctively, but they need to be taught how to make a kill. This is why kittens reared on farms, where their mothers are more likely to hunt, often develop into the best mousers in later life.*

Killer cats: Lessons from mother

Although the urge to hunt is instinctive in cats, they vary in their eagerness for the chase and also in their prowess. Their early life is significant in this respect. Kittens that have been reared on farms or ranches, for example, where there is probably plenty of natural prey, are likely to be more avid hunters throughout their lives than those reared in the home. This is because kittens need to be taught how to hunt effectively by their mothers.

On the farm, the mother is likely to bring back prey for her offspring, even if she is being fed by the owner. Before long, the young kittens will start to play with her dead quarry, patting it with their paws and then jumping on it. Later, as they approach independence, they will start to accompany her on hunting expeditions.

The actual hunting pattern is identical among both wild and domestic cats. There are few animals that are more patient than cats when they are in pursuit of prey. A cat will position itself quietly near to a burrow, for example, waiting for the occupant to emerge, while using whatever cover that might be available to conceal its presence.

Opposite *Lions hunt as a pack to run down large prey, seeking a weak or young victim. Lionesses rather than male lions are usually involved in hunting.*

Practical Pointer

Many of the stalking and pouncing postures used by cats when hunting can be seen when they are playing with toys (see page 86), and are also obvious when a group of kittens is playing together.

Powerful pounce

When the prey does emerge, the cat will have to make a split-second decision on when to pounce. If it moves too early or too late, its quarry is likely to escape. This is where experience is important, particularly when prey is hard to locate. It is quite common for young cheetahs, for example, to starve simply because they have not acquired the necessary hunting skills. In fact, even experienced farm cats only achieve a successful kill in less than a quarter of all attempts; not surprisingly, birds escape more often than rodents.

Cats tend to pounce using just their front legs, keeping their hindquarters on the ground to improve their balance, which can help them to hold onto their quarry if necessary. After catching its prey, a cat will often not kill the creature immediately, but will instead torment it for a while. The unfortunate mouse, for example, may be allowed to run off a short distance before being seized again by the cat, and then ultimately killed by a bite to the neck.

BASIC INSTINCTS • Choosing prey

By flattening itself against the ground and moving slowly, the cat has the best hope of reaching its quarry undetected. Like their wild relatives, domestic cats are selective about their quarry, typically ignoring voles for example, while hunting birds eagerly. They will catch frogs quite readily, but ignore toads because of the poison on the skin of these creatures. This is a lesson learned at an early stage in life by many kittens, which may be left drooling severely, having seized a toad. If you suspect that your cat has been poisoned by a toad, contact your veterinarian for advice.

Domestic cats may sometimes eat their quarry, adopting a method similar to that used by their wild relatives. Mice are consumed whole and head first, in order to be swallowed more easily; in the case of a bird, the cat may attempt to scratch the feathers off beforehand. Shortly after the mouse has been partially digested, its fur is likely to be regurgitated.

As seen in this serval, the patterning of wild cats makes it easier for them to move undetected through the landscape. This is known as disruptive camouflage.

CLIMBING

Many cats, even the larger species, will climb on a regular basis. Leopards, for example, will cache food in trees out of reach of other carnivores which are unable to climb. Even cat species that normally stay on the ground, such as lions, will climb on occasion, simply to find a shady place. The rusty-spotted cat goes one stage further, in that it will even hunt for birds and other creatures off the ground.

Cats move in a sure-footed manner when they walk along branches. Note the way in which this cat has spread its toes to help support its weight and also to give it extra balance.

Flexibility and balance

The flexible backbone of the cat helps it to climb. Domestic cats will climb as readily as their wild relatives, indoors and out. If deprived of an opportunity, they may inflict damage by attempting to climb up curtains. A cat that is kept inside permanently should have a suitable climbing frame for this purpose.

Ups and downs

Cats rely heavily on their claws to gain a foothold on the tree or fence post when climbing. A cat will leap up and then cling on with its front legs, using its powerful hind limbs to assist its ascent. When jumping off the ground, cats can reach a height of up to five times their own body length. They will then climb cautiously, with their body weight being supported by their hind legs.

Coming down again in due course is not so easy. Domestic cats, unlike their more arboreal cousin the rusty-spotted cat, cannot simply turn and clamber down a tree head first. Instead, they will begin by backing down, until within jumping distance of the ground, when they swivel their bodies and leap down. This is because their claws are not sufficiently flexible to assist their descent, while the hind limbs cannot support their weight from above, only from below.

If a cat does lose its grip while climbing, however, it is usually able to survive without serious injury. This is thanks to their rapid reflexes. Sensory information obtained from the semicircular canals in the inner ear is conveyed and processed very rapidly by the brain, which enables the cat to start swiveling its body very quickly if it falls. This in turn ensures that it will

Practical Pointer

Declawing a cat severely handicaps its ability to climb effectively and can therefore place your pet in danger, should it be confronted with an angry dog, for example. This surgery, known as onychectomy, is banned in a number of countries. If you have a declawed cat, it must not be allowed to range freely, but should be kept in the home for its own safety.

land on its feet. The pads on the feet make contact first and act as effective shock absorbers, dissipating much of the force of the impact. The tail also has a part to play, balancing the body and preventing the cat from twisting around too far.

It is not unknown for cats to survive falls from hundreds of feet above ground, although in these cases the momentum of the impact is such that the lower jaw is still likely to hit the ground, resulting in a fracture.

When simply jumping down off a roof, for example, the cat will start by standing right at the edge and placing its front feet in a position to jump, having extended its body downward as far as possible to minimize the impact with the ground. The cat always lands on its front feet, followed rapidly by its hind legs, which help to cushion the impact.

Practical Pointer

If you live in an upper-floor apartment with a cat, always make sure that the windows are safely closed — or, in hot weather, screened in some way — and that there are no gaps on a balcony through which a young kitten could fall to the ground.

BASIC INSTINCTS • Taking to the trees

The climbing ability of wild cats varies through the family. Some species, such as the rusty-spotted cat, regularly hunt in the trees, while other cats, such as the leopard shown above, will drag kills up off the ground, so that they are out of reach of other predators, such as jackals.

At the other extreme, lions rarely climb, nor do cheetahs. Especially where cover on the ground is rather sparse, however, lions may occasionally decide to retreat up into the trees, to avail themselves of the shade beneath the canopy of leaves when the sun is at its hottest.

Cats have no difficulty in walking across a sloping roof, using their sharp eyesight to pick the best route.

If it does start to slip, the cat can rely on the assistance of its claws to help maintain a foothold.

When it is ready to jump down, the cat positions itself in such a way that it can leap down onto a clear area below.

INTERACTION AND PLAYING

Cats have a playful side to their natures, which is most clearly seen in kittens. In reality, all cats will continue to interact in this way with their owners well into old age, particularly if they have been encouraged to play from a young age.

Communicating with humans

The way in which cats relate to and communicate with each other is mirrored in the way that they communicate with us. They have evolved behavioral patterns, not seen in their wild counterparts, that are specifically appropriate for a domestic environment.

When two cats that get along well meet, they approach with their tails raised and slightly curled forward at the tip. They will then pause and sniff the nose of the other cat, and, depending on the circumstances, they may then curl up and rest together.

In a typical "seeking attention" display, this cat is weaving around the legs of its owner. There may be food about!

A cat will also greet its owner with raised tail, but in this case it will weave around that person's legs, particularly when seeking food. It will often curl up next to the person, resting its head in his or her lap and starting to purr. If ignored when it wants something, to go out, for example, the cat will resort to uttering different sounds depending on the urgency of its request. Certain breeds, such as the Siamese, are far more vocal than others, such as the Russian blue, which tends to be naturally quiet.

The well-tempered cat

Sometimes the enthusiasm of a cat can become overwhelming. Do not allow it to jump up at you, because this may damage clothing, and is likely to be painful. Push your cat down, walk away, and ignore it for a period. Before long, it should realize that its behavior is unacceptable, and confine itself to weaving around your legs.

Cats are creatures of habit, and will soon establish a routine. Feeding is anticipated at a set time, and if you are late, your cat will not hesitate to pester you. Outdoors, cats have spots where they will sleep at certain times of the day when the weather is good. It is not good to allow your cat to roam freely at night, because this is the time when it is most likely to be involved in an accident or a fight. Encourage the cat to come in at dusk on a regular basis. Cats will soon recognize their name, and respond if they are likely to receive food or a treat when indoors. The cat's lifestyle is suited to owners out at work. Your cat will settle down and sleep for much of the day waking up in the evening when it will want your attention.

Exits and entrances

As domestic cats have become more numerous in urban areas, where space is limited, they have evolved complex means of keeping out of each other's way. They develop a network of invisible paths marked by scents, allowing them to cross a neighbor's territory without fear of attack (see page 74). Careful timing and time-sharing of territory help to avoid flash points. One cat may be seen in the area in the morning, to be replaced by another later in the day. It is possible for one cat to determine how recently another cat has passed through an area, because they leave traces of scent from the sweat glands that are located between the paws.

Cat flaps

Persuading a young kitten to take its first steps outside can be difficult, but once it is used to going out, you will find it useful to install a cat flap, to allow it to move in and out on its own. This is to be recommended especially if you are out at work during the day.

There are a number of different designs of cat flaps on the market, ranging from a simple swinging flap to sophisticated designs which will allow only your cat to pass through. These are preferable, because otherwise you can find your home invaded in your absence by other cats, which may choose to soil indoors.

It is not generally difficult to persuade a cat to use a cat flap, because like their wild ancestors, they will willingly venture through relatively small gaps. Start by keeping the cat flap fixed open, with the cat inside. You can then go outdoors and call your pet to you from the other side. Carry out this process several times, so that ultimately the young cat moves in and out readily, without hesitation. Then repeat the lesson with the entrance closed, so your cat can master using the flap. It may help to hold the flap partially open at first and dangle a favorite toy to attract the cat's attention from the other side, encouraging it to push its way through the opening.

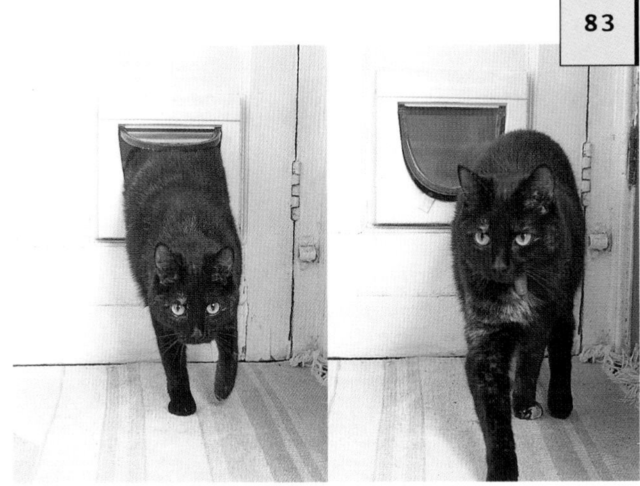

Above *Entrances: A young cat can be persuaded to use a cat flap by leaving it open and calling to the cat through the opening, with the flap held or tied out of the way. Be sure to position the cat flap so that burglars cannot reach any key in the doorlock above.*

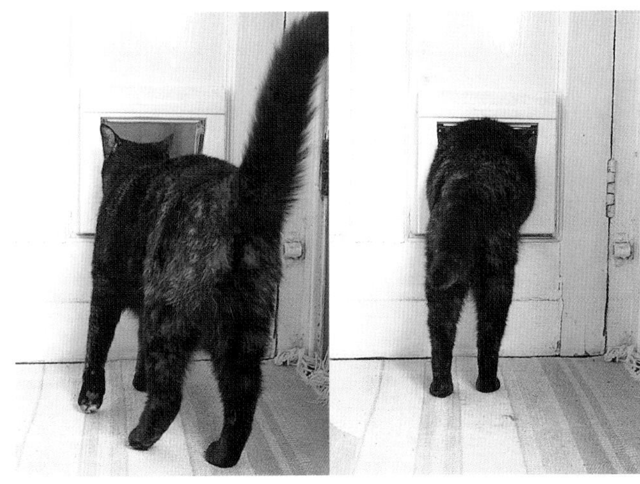

Above *Exits: If this procedure is repeated in the reverse direction, the cat will soon weave its way in and out on its own, after which the flap can be lowered. Encourage your pet to continue coming through by calling it. The cat should then continue to use the flap without concern.*

Practical Pointer

If you do not have a cat flap that admits only your cat, avoid leaving food available in the kitchen while you are out. This would attract other cats in the vicinity, with the result that your cat could end up hungry!

Dogs and cats can live in harmony without problems, particularly if they are introduced at an early stage.

Cats and other pets

A cat must often learn to relate not only to other cats and to people but also to other kinds of animal. A young kitten may encounter other pets in the home and it will have to establish a relationship with them. As with a resident cat and a newcomer, it is not a good idea to begin by forcing an encounter between the animals — by placing a kitten alongside your dog, for example. Instead, allow them to come together in their own time.

Pets as prey

Domestic cats have not lost the hunting instincts of their wild relatives, and so it will be very important to protect a pet that could be the cat's natural prey from any risk of danger. Small mammals such as mice and hamsters will be particularly vulnerable, and it is not unknown for rabbits to also be attacked by domestic cats.

Protect such pets both in the home and outdoors by making sure that their quarters are secure and cannot be dislodged by a determined cat. Although a kitten may at first show little or no interest in a hamster, for example, do not be fooled; before long the cat will jump up onto a table in the hope of reaching the creature. Once it finally realizes that it cannot open the cage, however, the cat will probably lose interest.

Nevertheless, the experience may be disturbing for the hamster, particularly if it cannot burrow away from sight into its bedding, so keep a watchful eye on the two. Constantly keeping the cat away is not necessarily the answer, because once prevented it is likely to react by becoming more determined to reach the creature. Obviously, they should never be left alone together without supervision.

Beware of cats upsetting pets such as birds or small rodents, which are its natural prey. Even if the cat cannot reach them, its presence may cause stress.

Impress on children, in particular, that if they want to open the cage and allow their pet out — to clean its quarters, for example — they must first locate the cat, to prevent the risk of any accident. A cat can move faster than they can, and, in the resulting disturbance, seize a small animal and rush away with it.

Birds and fish

Pet birds are also obviously at risk from cats; and again, the whereabouts of the cat must be firmly established before the bird is allowed out of its cage. Many pet birds are overweight, with the result that they may not be able to fly as powerfully as their wild counterparts.

In the case of a bird, there is a further risk that the cat may be able to insert a paw through the bars of the cage. This could obviously harm the bird, although in the case of a parrot, the bird might well retaliate by using its sharp bill to inflict a painful bite on the cat's paw.

Outdoors, some cats will take an interest in the fish in a garden pond. The major risk periods will be during the fall and then again in the early spring, when the vegetation in the pond has died down, so that the water is clear, while the fish themselves are more sluggish because of the cold. Placing a special pond net over the surface will protect them.

Practical Pointer

If, in spite of your endeavors, the cat does manage to injure another pet, and particularly if it bites the animal, take the victim to your veterinarian. Even though the wound may appear superficial, the bacteria that are present in the cat's mouth can set up a deadly infection.

Some cats are attracted to ponds and seek to catch fish there. Vegetation in the pond will help to provide cover for the fish, but they become more vulnerable in winter when it dies back and the water temperature cools, slowing down their activity.

Cat toys

Although wild cats obviously do not have the opportunity to play with toys, those kept in zoos will often utilize climbing frames and other items provided in their quarters for behavioral enrichment. This is a reflection of the innate curiosity of the cat and of its playful instincts.

For domestic cats there is now a greater range of toys available than ever. You may need to visit a large specialty pet supply store, however, if you are looking for cat furniture, because of the size of these units.

Try to set a regular time each day to play with your cat, as this will improve your pet's fitness and possibly alert you to any health problems, such as slight lameness, that might otherwise be overlooked until they become more serious. In the case of kittens, you can use these periods of play for training as well (see page 90), persuading your pet, for example, to release a ball without scratching you. Do not abandon these regular play sessions as your cat grows older, since they are usually playful throughout their lives.

The cat's curiosity can be its undoing, resulting in injury in some cases. If this was a can of food, your pet could cut its leg on the rim; dispose of cans carefully.

Toys that can take it

When selecting toys for your cat, be guided by their likely durability. A wind-up mouse, for example, may appear a natural choice, but although your cat is likely to play with it, the fur covering could soon start breaking down, causing fibers to stick to your cat's tongue. The wheels themselves could also be damaged.

A simple ball is easy to clean if necessary, but choose a reasonably durable one which will not be damaged or punctured easily by the cat's teeth. Chasing and pouncing on a ball is similar to the way in which a wild cat will jump on its prey, and so such games can become quite rambunctious. Sisal toys are ideal for this simulated hunting, as they allow the cat to roll over and seize them with their claws, and they are exceedingly durable.

Cat furniture, in the form of cubes, climbing frames, and similar equipment, is particularly important for a cat that must live indoors on a permanent basis. They allow the cat to climb, hide, and act as it would if living outdoors. It is important that these units, particularly the covers, be easily washable, however, in case of an infestation of fleas.

Practical Pointer

If you are expecting visitors, encouraging a young kitten to play beforehand should mean that it is ready for a sleep by the time they arrive, so that it will not create a disturbance.

Homemade toys

Many cats prefer toys improvised from ordinary household items to purchased toys. Paper bags

are a perennial favorite, as are lengths of yarn. However, yarn is a little risky. If a length breaks off and gets wrapped around a tooth, it might trail down into the throat, causing the cat to choke. Children should therefore be discouraged from using it as a toy when playing with the cat.

If you have two young cats, you will find that they will often play together on their own. This is similar to the "rough and tumble" games observed with wildcat kittens in the period when they are effectively independent, but still living within the family group. Much of this type of play is geared to determining which cat is dominant, and such direct interaction is likely to decline as they grow older. It should be possible to play with both of them at the same time, particularly if they each have their own ball to chase.

Practical Pointer

Never tease your cat when your are playing a game with it, as this may cause it to scratch in frustration, or simply to lose interest. For example, if you are dangling a piece of string above its head, allow the cat to catch it after a moment or two.

Young tiger cubs will play together, engaging in mock fights. This appears to be aggressive, but injuries are rare. The young cats are honing their hunting skills.

LIFESTYLE

The lifestyle of cats is slow and deliberate, compared with the often frenetic activity displayed by dogs. This measured behavior is very apparent in wild cats, which may wait silently for hours for possible prey, or sleep for hours. The level of activity of domestic cats is influenced also by their environment.

Above *Cats will relax for long periods, in spite of the fact that they are supreme, versatile natural athletes, capable of running, jumping, climbing and even swimming in some cases.*

Catnaps

During the summer, they often laze in the garden, occasionally pursuing butterflies that may venture near them. Following the onset of winter, many cats prefer to spend much longer indoors, sleeping close to a fire. They can sleep so soundly that they may even singe their fur in this way. It is important therefore to ensure that there is an adequate barrier in front of the fire, to prevent any injuries of this type.

If your house is centrally heated, you may be able to deter your cat from lying too close to an open fire or occupying one of your chairs by providing a special hammock-style bed. These fit neatly and easily to the top of a radiator, allowing the cat to lie comfortably off the ground, close to the source of heat.

Both young cats and older cats will sleep for most of the day, although they wake for periods and go back to sleep — giving rise to the term "catnapping."

Sleeping patterns

The sleep pattern of cats varies greatly between individuals, being influenced predominantly by their lifestyle. A cat that is left alone for most of the day will tend to sleep throughout this period, waking up when its owners come home. This is one reason why cats have recently become so popular as pets; it is possible to leave them on their own without problems during the day if you have to go out to work.

Practical Pointer

Wash the cat's bed regularly, not only to prevent it from smelling but also to reduce the risk of parasites such as fleas multiplying.

Practical Pointer

Make sure that a new kitten is allowed sufficient periods of sleep, especially since kittens sleep longer than adult cats. Children, in particular, should be cautioned on this point.

When a cat has constant human company, however, its periods of activity will be similar to those of the person. Cats do not naturally sleep for long periods, but have sessions of activity that are broken by sleep. This is actually how the term "catnapping" originated.

Cats go through a series of different sleep patterns — similar, but not identical, to those in humans. The pattern starts with dozing. At this stage, the cat will be sitting with its head raised and eyes closed, although if distracted by a noise nearby, it will respond readily. If undisturbed, however, the cat will, within half an hour, start to display signs of deep sleep. Its body will relax, and it will roll over, becoming unresponsive to noise.

This is the stage at which its body may start to twitch. It is often called REM sleep, meaning "rapid eye movement," which is another characteristic of this phase of sleep. Unlike human REM sleep, this is the deepest level of sleep among cats. Kittens sleep only in REM mode for the first month of their lives; then the adult pattern of alternating sleep phases develops. Each period of REM sleep lasts for about seven minutes, and during this time the cat's brain is very active.

The cat then experiences a phase of lighter sleep, which continues for up to half an hour. This cyclical pattern is repeated until the cat wakes up. The reason why cats require so much sleep is unclear, but they will usually sleep for up to 16 hours every day, which is twice as long as most people spend asleep.

BASIC INSTINCTS • A hunting lifestyle

In contrast to their domestic relatives, wildcats will rarely feed every day. Small prey, such as rodents, are eaten instantly, being swallowed head first, so that the fur will slide smoothly down the throat.

In the case of the larger cats, which take bigger quarry, they will feed for a while and then often try to hide the remains of the carcass from scavengers, returning to the spot under cover of darkness to feed for several days, until the remains are putrid. This often requires them to drag the carcass some distance from the site of the kill, so as to disguise it more effectively. With lions, however, the openness of their surroundings (as can be seen above) makes such behavior ineffectual. Once they have eaten their requirements, other scavengers will then move in and strip the carcass, forcing the pride to make another kill in due course, rather than returning to it. The solitary leopard seeks to avoid loss of its food by retreating up into a tree, where it will be out of reach of many scavengers. The bleached bones of herbivores, occasionally found in trees, are usually the remains of leopard kills.

TRAINING

It is generally not possible to train cats to the same degree as dogs, largely because of their independent natures. Training entails persistent interaction between animal and owner, tacitly acknowledged as the leader of the pack. Cats — with the notable exception of lions — do not live in structured groups, and so do not recognize a leader. Nevertheless, cats can respond to training, especially if this begins while they are young — as shown by the performances of lions and tigers in circuses down the centuries.

Tackling problem behavior

In the case of domestic cats, one of the most important lessons that need to be learned is housebreaking (toilet training). This is reasonably straightforward in most cases, because cats are instinctively clean, even as kittens, and will use a litter box with relatively little encouragement.

When soiling does occur elsewhere in the home (whether it is urine or feces), you should clean it up thoroughly, not only cleaning the area with a special pet disinfectant but also using a descenting preparation to discourage the cat from returning to soil this area again.

Above *One of the best ways to prevent a cat from soiling a particular area of garden is to spray the animal with water. Cats dislike this, and will not be keen to repeat it, preferring to go elsewhere in future.*

Scent plays an important part in the lives of cats. This can create problems in the home. Clear up thoroughly afterward, to prevent further soiling at the same spot.

Practical Pointer

Be consistent with your pet. If you do not want it to sleep on furniture, for example, make sure that the kitten recognizes its own bed from the outset, rather than trying to stop it from jumping onto a sofa once it is older, which will be much harder.

If a breakdown in toilet training does occur, this is usually caused either by an underlying medical condition or, more commonly, by a territorial incursion by another cat.

Corrective measures

If your cat persists in behaving badly, for example, jumping onto work surfaces, or trying to catch other pets, then clearly you can move it elsewhere and scold it. This should correct the bad behavior in the short term — but not permanently. There is little to be gained by smacking the cat, and once upset, it may retaliate by either scratching or biting you.

Some owners give the cat a sharp tap on the nose with a finger if it misbehaves, but a more effective means of punishment is a water pistol. This is especially useful if the cat is lying in wait to ambush birds in the garden, approaching a bird table or other feeding station. As cats particularly dislike being squirted with water, you can drive your pet away from a distance.

A way of protecting the neighborhood wildlife from your cat is to obtain an elasticized collar with a bell. This will, for a time, alert the birds to your pet's presence as it tries to stalk them. Before long, however, the cat is likely to have adjusted its movements so that it can hunt without the bell's sounding. The tinkling of the bell could annoy the cat so it is only recommended if the cat is a determined hunter.

BASIC INSTINCTS • Training wild cats

Although cats are generally not as amenable to training as dogs, for centuries the larger cats, notably lions and tigers, have been trained to perform in circuses. As with all animals, this training is most likely to be successful if begun at an early age. Even so, the unpredictable nature of big cats such as lions and tigers may cause them to suddenly turn on and attack their trainer, for no apparent reason.

Male wild cats can prove to be especially unpredictable. In Africa, leopards have a reputation for being particularly dangerous, whereas cheetahs are regarded as much more kindly disposed toward people. In fact, in Asia it used to be commonplace for cheetahs to be kept and trained for hunting purposes, and they were even exercised on leads, somewhat like hounds. Akbar the Great (1542–1605), the first Mogul emperor of India, maintained an amazing collection of these animals.

Trophies

One rather distressing trait, which cannot normally be overcome easily, is when a cat returns with an animal or bird it has caught and brings this into the home. In some cases, the unfortunate creature may not even be dead. This behavior is equivalent to that of the mother cat bringing home food for her offspring — the cat is bringing you a gift, however repugnant you may find it.

Under such circumstances, you should simply remove the creature and ignore the cat. Hopefully, this will be sufficient to discourage a repetition, although this is unlikely. Scolding your pet under these circumstances may weaken the bond between you.

Training is not just a question of persuading your pet to behave properly, but also of encouraging it to come when called. This can be achieved most easily by beginning to call the cat when you feed it. Before long, the kitten will associate its name with a positive response from you, and once established, this bond between you should last for life.

Domestic cats, like wildcats, will generally seek to bury their feces, but in larger cats feces can be used as a territorial marker and so are deposited in prominent places, rather than concealed or buried.

Toilet habits

Most cats are fastidiously clean creatures, despite the fact that they use both their urine and feces as territorial markers. Wildcats will usually bury their feces, unlike the larger cats, and this trait is still apparent in the case of the domestic cat. This behavior may be an irritant to neighbors who are keen gardeners, however, because domestic cats will inevitably regard a recently dug area of earth as its own lavatory.

The cat will use its front paws to excavate a suitable hollow in the earth, then squat over it, and finally cover the site again, scratching the soil back. This can lead to difficulties if seeds or small seedlings have recently been planted in this piece of ground, because inevitably some of them will be disturbed. It is possible to buy harmless chemical deterrents at garden centers and similar outlets to keep cats away from specific parts of a garden, but the effectiveness of these is often compromised when it rains.

Litter boxes

Indoors, when starting out with a cat or kitten, you will find a litter box an essential piece of equipment, certainly until your cat can be let out into the yard or garden. Indeed, many cats continue to use a litter box, especially in bad weather, when the outdoor conditions are less appealing. There are a number of different designs on the market. Those provided with a hood will give your pet greater privacy and also prevent litter from being scattered around the room, as the cat digs into it.

An alternative is the basic box with a shielded area on top, which again should serve to prevent the cat litter from being scattered. It is important, especially with a kitten, that it can get into the litter box without difficulty, because otherwise it will soil elsewhere in the home. Start by placing the kitten on the litter every time it has finished eating, because this is when it is most likely to want to relieve itself. Before long, it will learn to use the litter box of its own accord.

It is a good idea to place a lining in the box before adding the litter, as this will make it easier to clean. Special plastic liners of the appropriate size may be available for this purpose; although alternatively, you can use layers of newspaper, which are more absorbent.

A variety of materials are marketed as cat litter. Cat litter is highly absorbent, but relatively heavy, and disposal can sometimes be a problem. Never simply tip soiled cat litter down the toilet, as it could cause an expensive blockage here. Wood-based pellets have become quite popular over recent years and are lighter than clay-based products.

Practical Pointer

Do not provide soil as a filling for the litter box, because this is likely to bring invertebrates into the home and will make your cat's paws muddy. Neither sand nor wood shavings are especially absorbent and are not suitable.

Practical Pointer

Cats should have proper cat litter, rather than some improvised substance, such as cut–up newspaper, because its particulate nature allows them to excavate it, just as they would dig in the earth. Makeshift litter is likely to be ignored and a potted plant chosen in preference.

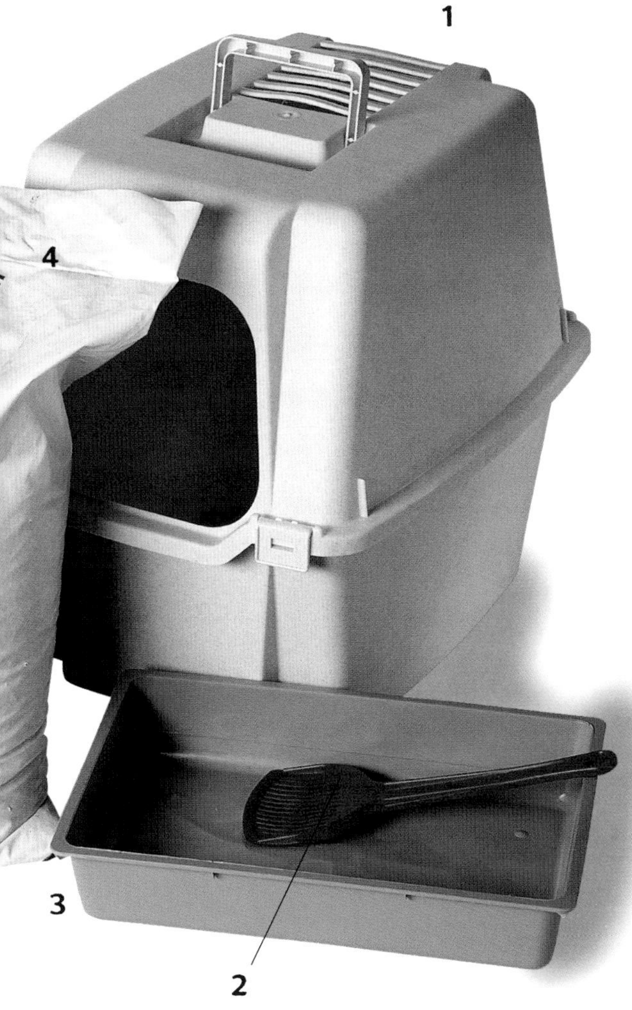

Above *The matter of finding the type of litter and litter container that suits your cat is often a case of trial and error. Shown here are a covered box style container* **1***, a scoop* **2***, a basic litter tray* **3***, and a bag of litter material* **4***. Dispose of the soiled litter as soon as possible, as cats are reluctant to use a dirty tray. Always wear gloves for this task.*

Above *Grooming is an extremely important activity in both wild cats and their domestic relatives. The rough surface of the cat's tongue helps to remove dirt. A cat will spend a lot of time cleaning its anal area after defecating.*

Cat litter is relatively expensive, but you need not usually discard the entire contents of the box everyday. Instead, use a special scoop (available from pet supply stores) to remove contaminated litter and solid waste. Do this as soon as possible on each occasion after the box is used, because otherwise the cat is likely to refuse to use it again. Do not simply rely on deodorants to disguise the odor, because cats will still tend to ignore a box that was soiled previously and has not been cleaned. If the box is scooped daily, you can change the litter once a week. Be sure to wash and dry the box thoroughly.

FEEDING &

HEALTH

Cats are hunters, and so depend on meat or fish as key parts of their diet. This may make life difficult if you are a committed vegetarian, but without this kind of protein, a cat is soon likely to develop symptoms of nutritional deficiencies. There is now no need to prepare fresh food for cats each day — a difficult task if the diet is to be nutritionally sound — for an excellent range of prepared foods for cats of all ages is now widely available.

The better understanding of the cat's nutritional needs which has led to the development of such diets is one of the major factors underlying the rapid rise in cat ownership in many countries. It has made looking after a cat very straightforward, leaving you free to spend more time enjoying the company of your pet. Associated advances in medical care have also ensured that cats are now living longer than ever before — often into their teens.

FEEDING

Cat Diets and Types of Food

All cats are active hunters, rather than scavengers. They will take a wide variety of prey, depending on their size and the environment where they are living. The diet of the wildcat varies depending on the types of animals who share its extensive territory, but it is centered mainly on rodents and birds of various types. Larger wild species such as lions and tigers will hunt bigger quarry; tigers pursue large herbivores, such as deer and sometimes even cattle.

A sad fact of keeping a cat is that it may catch a bird or rodent. The hunting instincts of domestic cats remain strong, but they can have problems killing their quarry.

Cats are opportunistic, however, and they will tend to eat whatever they can catch, which may range from small insects to turtles. Fish also form a prominent part of the diet of a number of species. Domestic cats are therefore unusual in readily eating prepared foods. Nevertheless, there are few fussier eaters than cats, and should their food suddenly be changed, they may well starve themselves rather than consume this equally nutritious alternative. Equally, if the food is stale, it is likely to be ignored by the cat.

All cats rely primarily on their sense of smell to determine whether or not to eat a certain food. They will sniff cautiously at it before deciding whether to taste it. In the case of a cat that has been suffering from a respiratory illness, persuading it to eat normally can often prove very difficult, simply because its sense of smell is likely to be impaired.

Fresh foods

Although many owners now use prepared dried or canned catfoods for their pets, some still prefer to provide them with fresh foods. These should be cooked and allowed to cool down before being offered to the cat. Lungs, liver, and other types of organ meat (offal) are frequently used as cat food, but over time they are nutritionally inadequate.

Practical Pointer

While some wild cats will eat plant matter on occasion, especially when other food is in short supply, it is not possible to maintain any cat satisfactorily on a purely vegetarian diet. For proper nutrition a cat's diet must contain meat.

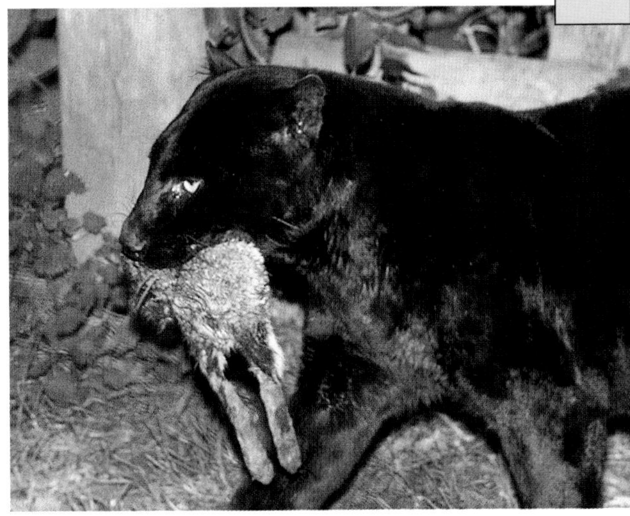

Cats may carry or drag their quarry some distance from where it was caught. This is an instinctive attempt to stop other predators from taking it.

Whereas wild cats eat their entire prey, the domestic cat fed on organ meat (offal) will not have access to the skeleton, which contains most of the body's calcium reserves. As a result, the cat will eventually develop skeletal weaknesses; this is particularly true in the case of kittens, which are growing rapidly. Nor is it only deficiency that can be harmful. Too much liver in a cat's diet will lead to a dietary excess of vitamin A, which can also lead to skeletal abnormalities. This can result in fusion of bones in the shoulders which is painful for the cat.

Cats will eat the whole animal, in the case of small prey, so that they receive the benefit of the calcium reserves that are contained in the skeleton.

While fresh foods can be used occasionally, particularly to tempt the appetite of a sick cat, it is very important to mix a suitable vitamin and mineral supplement with these foods, after consultation with your veterinarian, if you intend to use this type of diet for any length of time.

Although there is a popular myth that feeding raw meat to domestic cats can make them aggressive, this is untrue. But there is a possible risk — especially with the high volume of animals processed in modern meat-packing plants — that meat could be contaminated by a range of potentially harmful bacteria, such as *Salmonella*. There is a possibility that your cat could fall ill as a consequence, or might even acquire parasites. Cooking is therefore recommended in any event. The risk of such infection is lower in the wild, simply because the cat hunts and kills an individual animal and eats it almost at once, eliminating the risk of cross-infection.

Domestic cats will feed readily on prepared foods, but since they appear to establish their feeding preferences early in life, it can be difficult to get them to change from canned food to a dry diet for example. In many cases cats will starve rather than eat unfamiliar food.

Feeding: Prepared foods

The ready availability of prepared foods, containing all the essential nutrients required by cats, has been one of the major reasons for cats' burgeoning popularity as pets. The pet food manufacturers have invested huge sums of money to determine the correct formulation for their products, to the extent that there are now so-called "life stage" diets available, catering to the individual needs of kittens and adult and older cats. Even so, standard cat food is still widely used, and should not have any adverse effects on a cat's health.

Practical Pointer

If you need to store a partially used can of cat food, there are special plastic covers that are readily available to slip over the top of the can to prevent the odor of the cat food from spreading through the refrigerator.

Canned foods

Canned foods remain the food of choice with most cats, although this type of food is less convenient than the dry foods or semi-moist types and the cans themselves are heavy to carry and bulky to store for the owners. Canned food appears to be favored by many cats because it more closely resembles the cat's natural prey. Canned food has a much higher water content, often as much as 75 percent, compared with dried food which provides a more concentrated source of nutrients.

The feeding preferences of cats are usually quite firmly established early in life, so it is a good idea to offer a range of foodstuffs at this stage. You will then, hopefully, have a cat that is less fussy about its food in later life.

Dry foods

Dry foods typically have a water content of just 10 percent. They had a bad press in some countries in the early days, because of links between this type of food and the illness known as feline urological syndrome, or F.U.S. In cats affected by this problem (more males than females), the urine becomes relatively concentrated, and crystals form within the bladder. These then pass down the urethra, which connects the bladder to the outside. The result is not only a painful obstruction but also an impediment to the flow of urine. Rapid veterinary treatment is required to remove the obstruction, otherwise the cat's condition will deteriorate rapidly.

Today, the salt level of dry foods has been increased, to encourage cats fed on this type of diet to drink more fluid, reducing the likelihood of their developing F.U.S. In addition, the level of magnesium, suspected as the key culprit in the formation of these crystals, has been significantly lowered. In fact, it is now actually lower in dry foods than in many other foods fed to cats, such as sardines.

There are a number of advantages to using dry food. For one thing, the cat's teeth and gums are less likely to accumulate tartar. Dry food is also less likely to attract flies than canned or fresh food — a considerable advantage when the weather is hot. It is also much easier to store, because an opened bag or box does not have to be refrigerated.

This type of food is therefore ideal for "demand" feeding, as it can be left out throughout the day without risk of deterioration, provided that it stays dry. This is ideal for people who are living alone, as you can be sure that your cat will have food available, even if you are late coming home. Unlike dogs, cats rarely overeat when they are provided with free access to food, because their relatively high fat intake, which tends to slow down the emptying of the stomach, means that their appetite is quite rapidly satiated. The other type of prepared food is the semi-moist food, which combines the characteristics of both canned and dry foods. These foods are relatively light and are supplied in envelopes. They have a moister texture than dry foods, as their name suggests. Their water content is typically around 35 percent, and they contain additives to ensure that they do not dry out or turn moldy. Beware: Many semi-moist foods contain a lot of sugar that your cat does not need.

Practical Pointer

Do not simply keep adding new food on top of old, even when using dry or semi-moist food. Encourage the cat to empty its bowl; and wash this regularly, so that it remains clean.

*It is vital to wash the food bowl after each meal, whether you give your cat dry food **1**, canned food in jelly **2**, or semi-moist food **3**. Cats are fastidious about eating freshly presented food. Wash the bowl separately from household plates, rinse and dry before refilling, especially if you are giving dry food to your pet.*

Feeding routine

Whereas domestic cats should be fed once or twice a day, in accordance with the manufacturer's instructions on the food you are using, their wild counterparts often do not have the opportunity to eat on a daily basis. Several days may elapse before they make a kill. When quarry is plentiful, however, they will hide food, either in trees or on the ground, seeking a secluded spot where it will, hopefully, not be found by scavengers. The cat can then return here to feed over the course of several days.

Domestic cats will sometimes display similar behavior — particularly when offered fresh food, such as offals or a piece of cooked chicken (from which the bones should first be removed). They may then prove to be messy eaters, pulling the food out of their bowl and onto the floor, or even carrying it off to another part of the home or outdoors. Cutting the food into relatively small pieces is therefore advisable, to assist the cat as it eats and prevent the "takeaway" behavior.

Cats are not adverse to stealing food off plates, often jumping on to surfaces to reach it, so never leave any meat or fish accessible when you are out of the room.

BASIC INSTINCTS • Catching

In the case of wild cats, there is a real risk that other scavengers will be attracted to the site of a kill, resulting in the cat losing its meal. This is why many cats resort to dragging a carcass up into trees, where it will be out of reach of wild dogs , which cannot climb up there. The cat will eat its fill, and then return over the course of the next two or three days to continue feeding. It will then start looking for its next meal. Where the carcass cannot be dragged into a tree, it may be hidden in vegetation.

A kitchen can be a busy thoroughfare, and so may be an unsuitable place to feed your cat, especially if it seems to be nervous. A quieter spot outdoors may be preferable in fine weather. If your cat is a messy eater in the home, there are special wipe-clean mats available to place under food bowls.

Suitable dishes

Choose a food bowl that has a firm base to prevent the contents from being spilled if the cat treads on it. A suitable range of bowls for this purpose is available from most pet supply stores, but bear in mind that plastic bowls are more likely to be scratched badly over a period of time, and bacteria could multiply in these areas. Although stainless steel bowls can be washed easily, these containers tend to be quite lightweight, so they may be overturned readily. A sturdy earthenware or thick glass bowl makes the best food bowl.

Develop a routine for feeding your cat, starting with the feeding regimen to which it is already accustomed and sticking to the same food at first, to lessen the likelihood of any digestive upsets. Changes to your cat's routine can then be introduced gradually, after two weeks or so.

If you are using canned food, it is important to allow the contents to come to room temperature if taken out of the refrigerator, because cats dislike cold food. They will instinctively eat prey immediately after killing it, and so prefer to feed on meat close to body temperature. In fact, cold food may be ignored, so if your cat is a fussy eater, a little hot water or even gravy will raise the temperature.

Practical Pointer

Never wash the cat's bowl along with your own dishes, or use the same brush or cloth to clean it. This is unhygienic and could cause members of the family to become ill.

Domestic cats are not above investigating every option in search of interesting things to eat.

Loss of appetite

Keep an eye on the amount of food that your cat is eating, because loss of appetite may be an early indication of illness. This can be harder to gauge if you have more than one cat, however. It is also difficult to judge what your cat eats if you leave food accessible throughout the day outdoors, where other cats may come along and eat it.

There can be a number of other causes for a cat's loss of interest in its food, ranging from a change of diet to alterations in its environment. Even changes in the weather or thunderstorms especially may have an adverse affect. It is also possible that your cat could have found an alternative source of food, which it prefers, at a neighbor's home. This is especially likely should your cat disappear for relatively long periods during the day.

Providing a meal, or at least a light snack, last thing at night may help to encourage your cat to return indoors then, where it will be much safer than out roaming the streets.

Try to persuade your pet into this habit, so that even on a warm summer's night it will come back readily when called.

Drinking

All cats drink in a similar fashion, using their tongues like ladles, to lap up fluids. The tongue itself is flexible and curls at the tip for this purpose. In the wild, cats do not have a high requirement for water, simply because of the high water content of their prey — typically around 70 percent — which they can absorb into their bodies as part of the digestive process.

Many domestic cats also appear to drink very little. A cat feeding on canned or fresh food is likely to need only about 1oz (30ml) of water to meet its daily requirement. By contrast, those eating dry food should be drinking around 7oz (200ml). Otherwise their urine will inevitably become more concentrated; this increases the likelihood that salts will be precipitated in the urinary tract, causing symptoms of feline urological syndrome (F.U.S.). Therefore, you should always offer a bowl of fresh drinking water (although some cats will tend to ignore this, preferring instead to drink from puddles or garden ponds). As with food bowls, the water container should be secure, so that it will not tip over easily, spilling the contents.

Cats that are kept indoors will obviously not have the same opportunities to drink as their free-roaming counterparts, and may seek water in other parts of the home. Although attempting to drink droplets from a tap will not

The cat's tongue acts rather like a ladle when it drinks, with its tip serving to pick up the fluid at this stage.

Wildcats are forced to come to waterholes to drink, often at dawn or dusk. At this stage, especially after a recent kill, they will ignore other prey animals nearby.

Practical Pointer

Never be tempted to give a sick cat a dose of medicine in its drinking water, as the cat will be unlikely to consume enough water for the medicine to have a beneficial effect.

be harmful, other sources, particularly the toilet bowl, can be positively dangerous. Aside from the possibility that the cat could fall into the bowl, there is also the risk that it could ingest bleach or similarly harmful chemicals, and possibly pick up an infection, so be sure to keep the cat away from the toilet.

Practical Pointer

There is no need to let drinking water stand, to allow chlorine or similar chemicals to dissipate, before offering it to your cat. It can be supplied straight from the tap.

Milk

If given a choice, many cats will prefer to drink milk rather than water, although this is certainly not essential. Milk does contain important nutrients, such as calcium, but there is no need to offer the cat milk on a regular basis, because such ingredients are to be found in its normal diet.

In fact, not all cats are able to drink milk. Some, especially those of oriental origin, such as the Siamese, lack the necessary enzyme, called lactase, to break down the milk sugar, called lactose. As a result, this sugar will ferment in the cat's intestinal tract, causing diarrhea.

Should your cat be affected in this way, you can still provide it with milk if you wish, since special milk for cats is now sold in cartons in pet supply stores and some supermarkets. It contains only a very low level of lactose, so it will not endanger the cat's health. Once the carton has been opened, it needs to be stored like ordinary milk in the refrigerator.

Give your cat only the amount of milk it is likely to drink at a single sitting, because it will sour rapidly, especially in hot weather, and will then be ignored. A saucerful should be sufficient for most cats, although the milk may be better provided in a small bowl, where it is less likely to be spilled.

Although it is often believed that cats love milk, this is not strictly true — milk can make some cats ill, causing them to have diarrhea.

HEALTH

Neutering

In the wild, cats tend to have a fairly defined breeding season, with northerly wildcat populations only breeding when conditions are most favorable. Domestic cats are far more prolific.

Cats should never be allowed to breed unless you know that you can find a good home for the kittens or are prepared to look after them yourself.

One of the major advantages of neutering, aside from preventing unwanted kittens, is that it is likely to result in cats' becoming less aggressive, particularly in the case of males. This is actually because they slip lower down the social order, and are not perceived as rivals to the same extent by intact males.

Neutering a male cat involves castration — removing the testicles. In females the process is called spaying and consists of removing the ovaries. Surgery is more complex in the case of the female cat, because the abdomen has to be opened. There are two possible approaches, with the incision being made either on the flank or in the midline underneath the body.

In the case of pointed breeds, such as the colorpoint longhair or the Siamese, midline surgery is often preferable, because otherwise the new hair that regrows is likely to stand out, compared with that elsewhere on the body. This is because the coloration of the hair in these breeds is influenced by the environmental temperature, and a bandaged area will be warmer than the surrounding areas.

Cats usually recover uneventfully from this surgery, although they should be discouraged from jumping, particularly the females, until the wound has begun to heal. For example, if the cat shows signs of wanting to jump onto a chair, lift it up instead. The stitches will need to be removed after ten days, if the cat has not taken them out itself by this stage.

When to neuter

The age at which the cat is neutered can have a definite effect on its appearance, particularly in the case of short-haired tom cats. As an unneutered male matures, its face becomes more rounded, as it develops jowls. A tom cat neutered early in life will not display this

Practical Pointer

Before surgery the cat must fast; the required number of hours will be specified by your veterinarian. Be sure to keep your cat indoors during the fast, so that there is no risk of its slipping out and finding food. A cat with food in its stomach might vomit during surgery and choke to death.

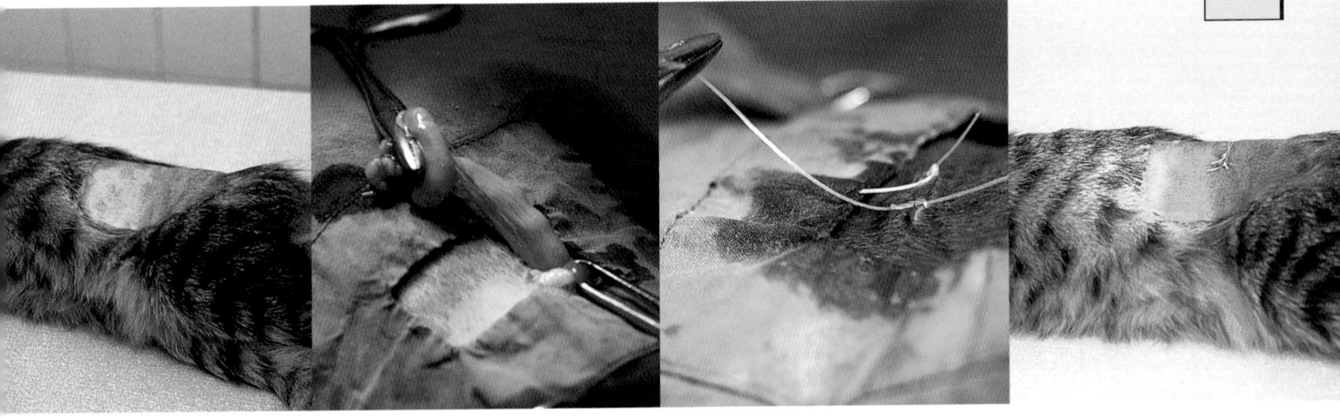

Neutering of a female cat, called spaying, is a fairly straightforward procedure, from which the cat recovers rapidly. The incision is normally made on the flank although in some cases it may be made on the underside of the body. The horns of the uterus are removed. The site of the incision is then sutured, with the stitches being removed around ten days later. The hair soon regrows over the site of the surgery.

masculine feature; it is also highly unlikely to spray urine as it grows older. This is because, being deprived of its testicles, it lacks the male sex hormone, testosterone, which is largely responsible for these effects.

Neutering is usually carried out when cats are between five and six months old, but it can take place later in life. Neutering a pregnant female is not advisable, because of the increased risk of complications. Internal hemorrhaging can be a problem although it is not always possible to know definitely when a cat is in the early stages of pregnancy.

If you acquire an older cat, you can tell whether it has been neutered, because its testicles will be missing; but this can be much harder to ascertain in the case of a female cat whose origins are unknown. In such cases, however, you may be able to detect a slightly raised ridge of skin under the fur on the flank, where the wound healed, or, alternatively, a similar area in the midline. If you are in any doubt it is advisable to ask your veterinarian when you take the cat for its first check-up, because it is important to ascertain without delay if your new pet is able to have kittens.

BASIC INSTINCTS • Effects of neutering

Neutering can affect both the personality and the appearance of the cat. This is shown most markedly in male lions by the disappearance of their manes in those neutered after attaining maturity. In zoos, where over-production of big cats can be a problem, new chemical methods of suppressing reproductive activity, which do not have this effect on the mane, are therefore used to control their numbers, in preference to neutering.

The changes to a cat's appearance following neutering are caused by hormonal alterations in the body, resulting from a fall-off in the output of sex hormones. This has both temperamental and physiological effects; neutered animals tend to be more docile and less active and they are also more prone to weight gain. In addition, their lifespan may be increased, because of their less aggressive disposition.

Diseases

In areas where they range over large territories, wild cats are less likely to encounter infections than their domestic cousins. But where groups of wild cats live in close proximity to each other, as is the case with lions, whose territories may also be crossed by other wild cats such as cheetahs, outbreaks of disease do occur, and these can decimate cat populations.

Rabies

In areas where the rabies virus occurs — which is most of the world, apart from islands such as Great Britain, Iceland, Australia, and Hawaii — this deadly disease can be spread from wild mammals of all types to domestic cats. It is therefore advisable, if you live in a region where rabies does occur, to have pets vaccinated as a precautionary measure, particularly since humans that are bitten by rabid animals can

Cats that live in groups as at this rescue home, are especially vulnerable to illnesses. Respiratory diseases are quite common among cats.

die from this infection, if they do not receive prompt treatment.

Vaccinations have helped significantly to eliminate many of the killer diseases that can afflict cats, such as feline infectious enteritis, feline rhinotracheitis, and feline calicivirus disease. It is important to revaccinate on a regular schedule, because cats can contract these diseases if they do not receive booster shots. These normally have to be given

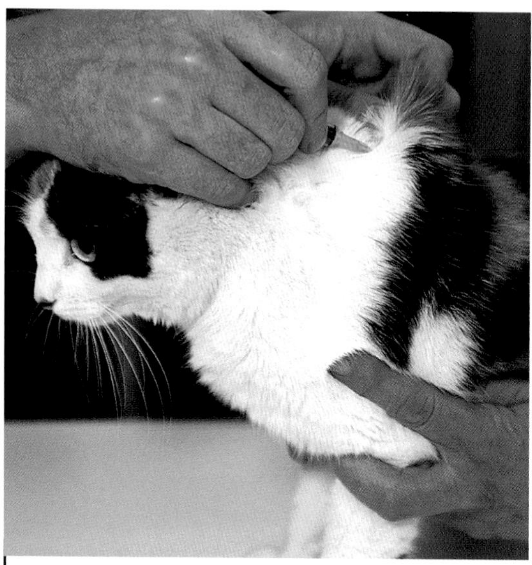

Practical Pointer

It is not normally necessary to have the vaccinations for each disease administered separately. The routine vaccines can usually be given in single shot combinations, which helps to make the experience less stressful for your pet.

annually, once the cat has finished the initial course of injections.

Unfortunately, many owners do not protect their cats, and so infection can spread rapidly through an area, particularly if there are colonies of feral cats in the neighborhood. These may be accustomed to scavenging for food in areas where domestic cats also roam, making the spread of infection more likely. In places where there is a high density of cats this risk is inevitably high.

One of the significant advances in recent years has been the development of a vaccine that affords good protection against feline leukemia virus (FeLV). This, too, can be transmitted very easily by bites and scratches, with the virus being spread in the saliva, so cats that fight regularly will be especially vulnerable.

FeLV is also present in the urine and feces of infected cats, but fortunately it does not survive for very long in the environment. Although feline leukemia virus represents no hazard to people, both wild and domestic cats are at risk and will readily succumb to this virus, which causes both leukemia and tumors affecting the lymphatic system.

Unfortunately, the feline immunodeficiency virus (F.I.V.) has no vaccine or cure. It attacks the immune system and may cause anemia, while lowering the general resistance to infection. It is spread in the saliva of cats.

BASIC INSTINCTS • Viral threats

Susceptibility to viruses varies in populations of wild cats. There is evidence, for example, that wild cats from parts of South America may have greater natural resistance to the effects of "cat flu" than domestic cats. It is also a puzzle as to why nearly all of the lions tested in the Kruger National Park in South Africa show signs of infection with feline immunodeficiency virus (F.I.V., also sometimes called Feline AIDS), with the level of infection there having risen by roughly a third over the past two decades, yet the lions themselves appear quite healthy.

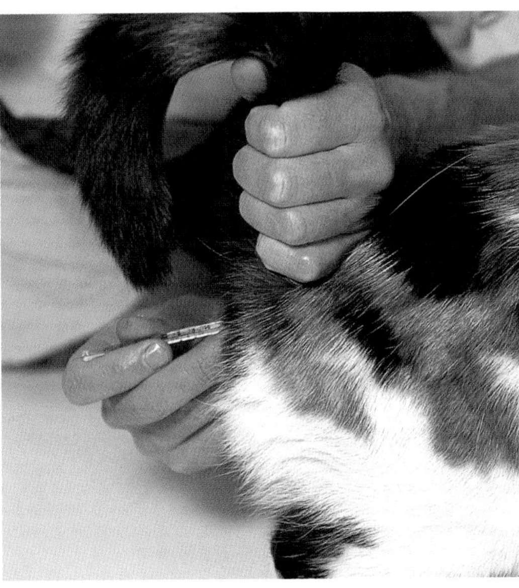

Vaccinations can now offer effective cover against the majority of serious feline viral illnesses, but booster jabs must be kept up to date for full protection.

Practical Pointer

Do not lose your cat's vaccination certificate. Not only will this tell you when your cat is due for a booster, but it will also be required if you should take your cat to a cattery. The staff will expect to see proof that your cat is fully immunized. Should you lose the certificate, ask your veterinarian for a replacement.

The third eyelid is clearly seen here — this is a sign of loss of condition, caused by the eyeball effectively shrinking back into the head, enabling the so-called "haws" to protrude across the eye. It is usually hidden.

Breed-specific problems

Domestic cats suffer from far fewer congenital problems than dogs. This may be partly because they have remained relatively constant in terms of size, and so their skeletal system has not been subjected to such alterations in shape. Nevertheless, some of the changes that have been brought about by selective breeding can be a cause for concern.

The munchkin

The short-legged munchkin, for example, a newcomer on the U.S. cat scene, has aroused considerable controversy. This is the first time that the proportions of the domestic cat have been modified in this way — although similar changes have been seen for centuries in the breeding of dogs, giving rise to such breeds as the dachshund and the basset hound.

The controversy stems partly from the fact that the shortened legs of the munchkin restrict the cat's ability to run and climb. Concerns have also been expressed that the joints may also be weakened, and be more prone to arthritis, but this does not appear to be the case as yet.

Above *Deafness can be a problem associated with blue-eyed white cats, for which there is no possible treatment. The cause is a congenital absence of part of the hearing apparatus.*

Supporters of the munchkin argue that this is not a freely living cat but a breed destined to be kept as a pet. In effect, this is one of the few breeds that have moved away from the original blueprint of the Felidae, and in effect represents a further step toward total domestication, in which the animal is no longer well adapted to living free.

Left *Tortoisehell cats are invariably female, but on the very rare occasions when males do crop up, they are sterile because of a genetic quirk, resulting in their having an extra chromosome in their genetic make-up.*

The sphynx

Another controversial breed is the sphynx, which is also known as the hairless cat, although it does show traces of hair on its body. This breed, which also has counterparts in the dog world, is more vulnerable than other cats both to cold and to the effects of sunburn.

Both the munchkin and the sphynx are mutations that first appeared in litters of otherwise normal cats. They have then been bred to preserve their distinguishing features. Selective breeding of this type is a relatively recent phenomenon — a result of the show scene. Specific standards, describing the required features, are laid down for the different breeds, and are used for judging entrants in each category.

This is not to imply that the cat's appearance will be static if nature is allowed to take its course, as can be seen by comparing photographs of Persian longhairs of the early twentieth century with those of today. Not only are these cats now larger in size, but their coats are significantly longer. A more significant change is that their faces are more compact, and, with their tear duct shortened dramatically as a result, these cats are likely to suffer from tear staining, with moisture running down the corners of their eyes. This needs to be wiped away regularly with damp absorbent cotton.

Practical Pointer

Domestic cats have evolved in accordance with their habitats. Those from the far north, such as the Norwegian forest, have long, dense coats to protect against the cold, compared with those originating in tropical areas, such as the Korat and the Siamese.

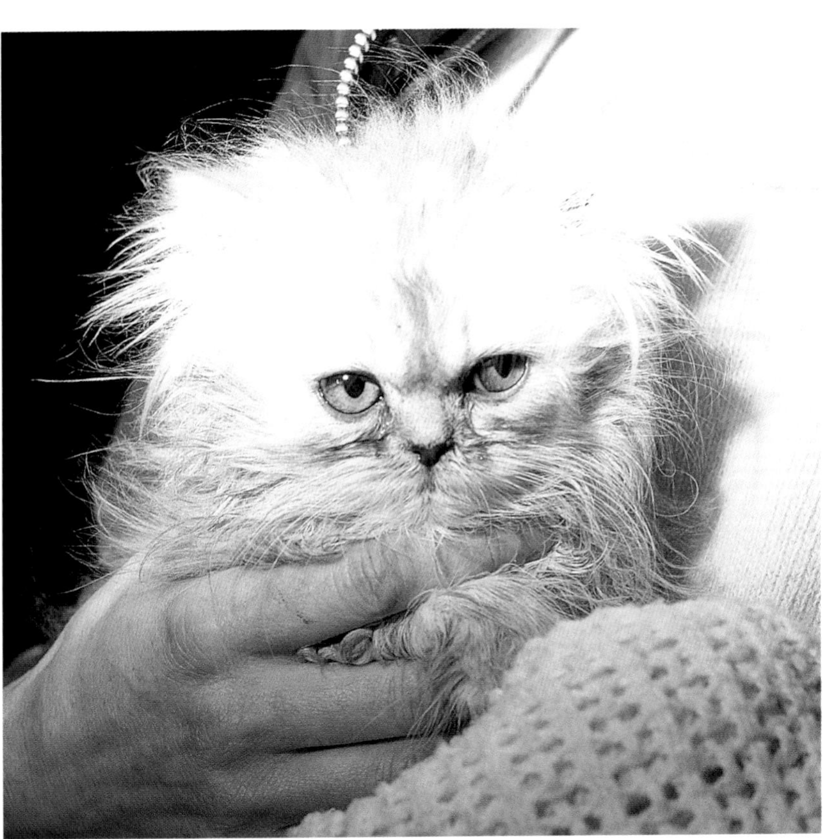

The shortened face seen in some breeds, such as the Persian can result in tear staining down the sides of the face, with the fur becoming matted, as seen here, because the drainage outlet from the eye can become blocked or may be more distorted than normal. These areas of fur will need to be cleaned with damp cotton (cotton wool) as a result.

Practical Pointer

Changes in the cat's appearance do influence their general care. Long-haired breeds require daily grooming and can be more susceptible to fur balls than shorthairs.

GENERAL HEALTH CARE

Domestic cats typically live longer than their free-ranging relatives, including feral cats. This is partly because they receive regular meals and are less subjected to stress, which can trigger heavy burdens of parasites and lead on to illness. They are more protected in the home and domestic cats can be vaccinated against the major infections that could kill their wild cousins.

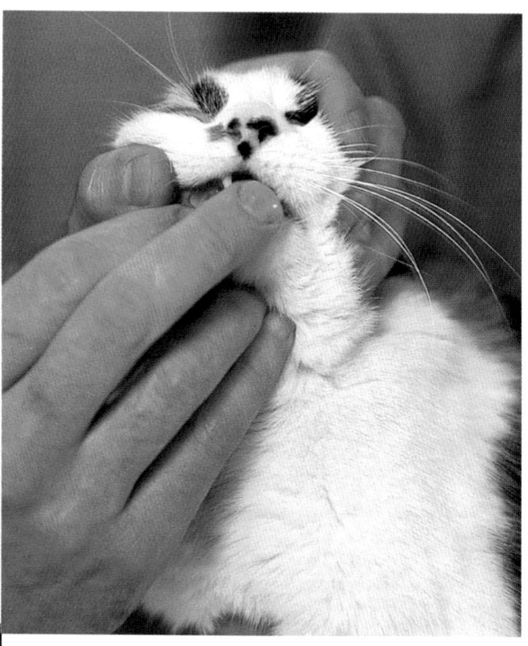

Practical Pointer

If you must give your cat a pill, first get someone else to restrain your pet; then pry its jaws apart with forefinger and thumb and place the tablet as far back down the throat as possible. Close the jaws and tickle the cat's throat to encourage it to swallow. Should this task prove too distressing for the cat or impossible for you to do, you may want to try a special pill dispenser, although this, too, has to be placed in the cat's mouth.

Looking out for symptoms

There are a number of general symptoms that you should be alert to, however, in case your cat does acquire an infection (although for most cats today, the risk of being run over by a vehicle is probably greater than succumbing to illness). Loss of appetite may be the first indicator of ill health, although this can also be caused by a number of other unrelated factors.

If the cat refuses to eat for more than a day or two, you should consult your veterinarian.

Other factors that are likely to be significant are whether your cat is vomiting or suffering from diarrhea, although this may not be immediately apparent in the case of a pet that regularly wanders outside.

The third eyelid

A specific indicator linked with ill health is the appearance of the third eyelid or nictitating membrane at the inner corner of the eye.

This third eyelid is present in both wild and domestic cats, but is usually hidden. Its appearance is actually not a sign of a specific illness, but shows a loss of condition. When the cat is in a normal state of health, the eyeballs are padded on a bed of fat. If the cat is no longer eating, this fat is broken down and utilized to provide energy and the eyes — no longer well cushioned — sink in their sockets, allowing the membrane to emerge over their surface.

Once the cause of this problem is corrected, the fat is deposited again, allowing each eye to return to its correct position, and the nictitating membrane then disappears.

Body temperature

Should you need to take your cat's temperature, arrange for someone else to hold your pet securely and firmly and smear the bulb of the thermometer with a safe lubricant such as petroleum jelly. Insert the bulb gently into the rectum for a minute or so. Healthy cats have a temperature of 101.5°F (38.5°C).

It is often said that a cat with a dry nose is ill, but this is not necessarily the case if it has been lying in a warm place, for example. If combined with other symptoms, such as lethargy and loss of appetite however, this is a sign that all is probably not well with your pet.

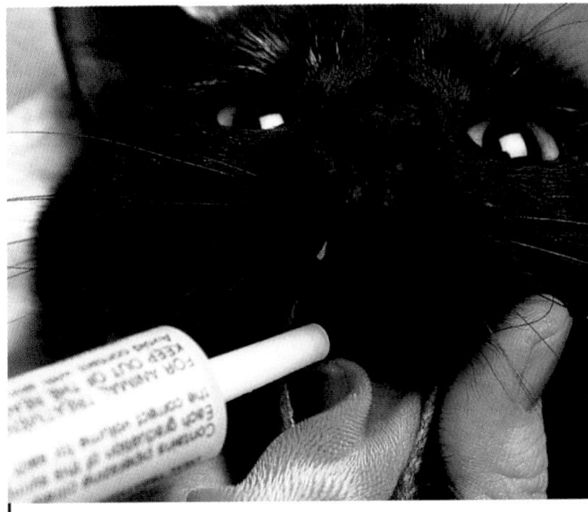

Practical pointer

When giving liquid medicine to your cat, use a syringe without a needle, so you can run the medication gently but consistently into the back of the mouth. If you squeeze too fast, however, the cat is likely to gag and retch and not swallow the medicine.

Above *Signs of illness may not always be diagnostic of a particular condition, but still indicate that there is something seriously wrong with your cat. The appearance of the third eyelids or "haws" — a whitish membrane across the lower part of the eyes closest to the nose, is a characteristic sign that your pet needs urgent veterinary attention.*

Above *Feral cats face a far more hazardous life than their domestic counterparts, and not surprisingly, they tend to have a shorter lifespan.*

External parasites and their control

Free-ranging cats are likely to acquire parasites at some stage in their lives. The period of greatest risk is during the warmer months of the year, although in a well-heated house, fleas can be a problem throughout the year. Wild cats are equally susceptible to these parasites.

Ticks

Ticks tend to be more common in agricultural rather than in urban areas, as their life cycle is linked to that of herbivores such as sheep and deer. Cats acquire ticks when walking in grassy areas.

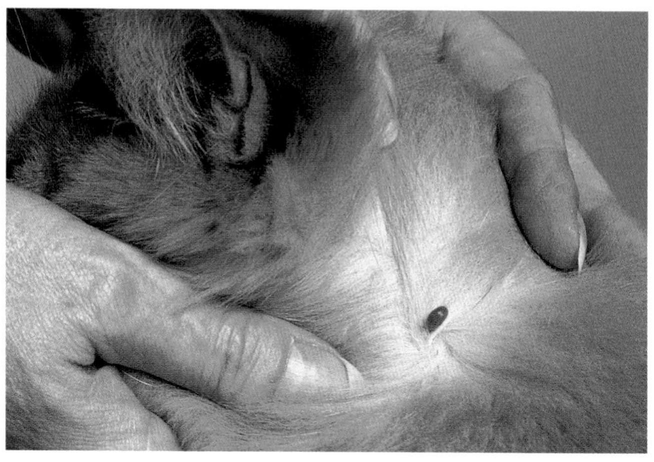

Above *A tick attached to the skin of a cat. While feeding on the cat's blood, these parasites can spread a number of diseases at the same time.*

Above *Flies can be a danger if a cat has an obvious skin injury or suffered from diarrhea, because they will lay their eggs at the site of the soiled fur.*

These parasites are relatively small when they first attach themselves to the cat. Anchoring themselves firmly into the skin with their mouthparts, they then suck the cat's blood and become noticeably swollen in size. Ticks carry deadly diseases that can spread to both cats and humans.

Regular grooming of your cat is the best way to locate these and other external parasites rapidly. Never be tempted, though, simply to pull a tick off. Its body will break away, leaving the mouthparts embedded in the skin, where they are likely to cause an infection. Instead, cover the tick thoroughly with petroleum jelly. This will block the breathing hole at the rear of its body, causing it to release its grip and fall off.

Practical Pointer

If you also have a dog, it too could be infested with fleas, so treat both pets at the same time. Read the instructions on the product carefully, checking that the treatment for your dog is safe to use on your cat.

Above *Flea dirt is visible here in the cat's fur. You are more likely to spot this than the actual parasites themselves. Grooming has a vital health care role, apart from keeping the cat's coat in good condition.*

Fleas

Fleas also spend only part of their life cycle on the cat. They, too, suck the cat's blood, with female fleas laying eggs that drop off and accumulate in large numbers in the cat's bedding. These then hatch into larvae, which live on the ground before changing into pupae. The fleas that subsequently hatch will then leap onto the cat and start to feed.

If your cat has fleas, you are more likely to see traces of flea dirt, visible as reddish–brown specks, than the fleas themselves. Place some of the specks on damp blotting paper; if they dissolve, creating reddish deposits, this is clear evidence of fleas. A special fine–toothed flea comb will be necessary to track down these parasites in the cat's coat. They often congregate along the back close to the tail.

A cat suffering from fleas will bite and scratch repeatedly at its coat, in an attempt to relieve the irritation. There is a real risk that your cat could become allergic to the fleas' saliva; in that case, only a single bite would be needed to cause a severe inflammatory reaction.

Fleas can also transmit a variety of harmful microbes, ranging from blood parasites to viruses, which are injected into the cat's body when they feed. Should the cat actually catch a flea and swallow it, there is a possibility that it could acquire a *Dipylidium* tapeworm infection, if the flea contained a cyst of this parasite. Effective treatment of fleas is therefore important, not least because other members of the family may also be bitten — although a cat's fleas will not live permanently on humans.

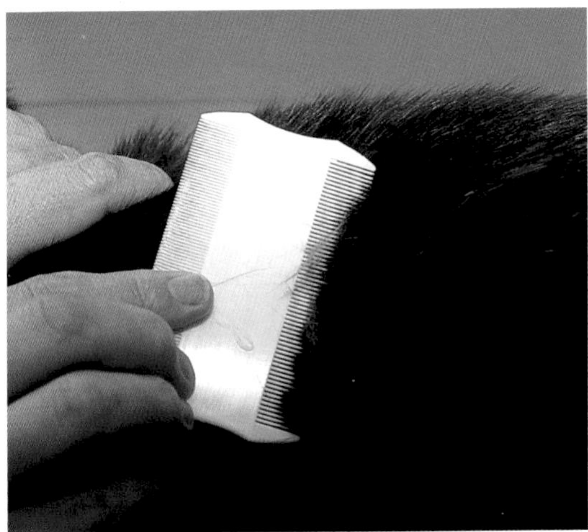

Above *Use a fine-toothed flea comb outside, so if fleas do jump off, they are less likely to reinfest your cat. Fleas slip through the teeth of an ordinary comb.*

Practical Pointer

Flea dips should only be used to deal with a heavy infestation, and then only on the advice of a veterinarian.

The new pills and liquids that are applied to the back of the neck have largely replaced flea collars and powders, as they are less toxic and more effective.

Cats eat grass as an emetic. This often indicates the presence of either intestinal worms or a furball.

Internal parasites and their control

The cycles of internal parasites are closely linked with the hunting abilities of cats. As a result, wildcats normally suffer much more from intestinal worms than their domestic relatives, although if the cat is in good health worms do not cause serious problems.

Roundworms

Domestic cats that hunt regularly are at greatest risk of encountering internal parasites. Once infected by the roundworm *Toxocara cati* — often acquired by eating rodents — an unneutered female cat may then go on to infect her young. This is because not all the eggs develop in the intestinal tract, some remain dormant in the cat's body. Once the cat starts lactating, these immature worms are then passed, via the mammary glands, into her milk and to the kittens, where they complete their development. A heavy burden of intestinal worms in kittens can lead to a pot-bellied appearance, combined with occasional diarrhea and a poor growth rate. It is therefore important to deworm kittens regularly, particularly as some of these parasites can be transmitted to people. In the case of kittens, treatment should begin at about three weeks of age, to eliminate parasites that may have been acquired from their mother's milk, and then be repeated roughly once a month, up until the age of six months. Cats that hunt should then be treated every four months. Cats living in catteries need deworming only once a year. Infection is widespread, with at least one in five domestic cats being infected at any time.

Tapeworms

Tapeworms can be distinguished from roundworms by their flattened shape. They too may be spread from prey, as well as by fleas. Treatment in this case is usually advised twice a year, from six months of age onward.

Depending on where you live in the world, there may be specific groups of worms that represent a threat to the health of your cat. For example, lungworms (*Aelurostrongylus abstrusus*) are common in parts of Scotland, but not elsewhere in Britain. This particular parasite cycles via snails and slugs. The larvae are voided in the cat's motions, and then these molluscs will pick up the infection if they ingest them. In due course, the cycle will be completed when a cat eats one of these infected invertebrates. Repeated coughing and retching are the characteristic signs of these particular parasites.

Climate may also be significant. Cats in the wetter parts of the United States, for example, are especially vulnerable to hookworm infections. The larvae in this case may be able to penetrate directly through the skin into the cat's body, and will then invade the intestinal tract. Anemia is a typical indicator of the hookworm infection; a cat suffering from it will appear lethargic.

Farm cats that hunt and eat rodents are at the greatest risk of suffering from internal parasites, because of their lifestyle.

Alternative health care

There is growing interest in alternative or complementary health care for domestic cats today. In the wild, of course, cats do not have the benefit of modern medication to cure themselves when they fall ill. Yet they will act in ways that clearly indicate an almost instinctive attempt to cure themselves — behavior also sometimes seen in domestic cats.

If a cat is suffering from a fur ball in its stomach, or a heavy accumulation of intestinal worms, it may chew and swallow fairly coarse stems of grass, which will act as an emetic. The obstruction is then cleared away and vomited out of the body.

Such behavior should not be confused with the tendency of some cats to eat tender shoots of grass on a regular basis; this may help to compensate for low levels of some B vitamins, notably folic acid, in their regular diet. At pet supply stores it is possible to buy grass growing kits for cats that stay indoors.

Herbalism and homeopathy

Herbalism relies entirely on the use of plants and plant extracts for treatment. In homeopathy, a much wider range of remedies is likely to be used. Some are of plant origin, but others are derived from animals or mineral extracts.

Herbalism utilizes the healing powers of plants in a way similar to conventional veterinary medicine, incorporating herbs in pills. Homeopathy entails a very different approach, based on the principle of treating "like with like." Homeopaths maintain that it is necessary to administer a substance similar to that causing the illness, in order to overcome the problem.

Practical Pointer

If your cat suffers from stress-related conditions, a range of alternative health-care options are available. Similarly, homeopathy can play a part not just in cases of illness, but also may assist with the healing of injuries as well as stress.

The practice of homeopathy originated with a German physician named Samuel Hahnemann (1755–1843). He found that taking cinchona bark — the source of quinine — would induce symptoms similar to those of malaria. Subsequently, however, it would also cure the symptoms of malaria. Hahnemann also discovered that by progressively diluting such substances, and shaking them — a process now called succussion — their potency was actually increased.

Aside from this fundamentally different approach to treatment, the homeopathic veterinarian will take a holistic view of a patient, rather than concentrating just on the symptoms that you have observed. By considering different aspects of the cat, including its temperament, for example, he or she will prescribe a homeopathic remedy specific to that animal — quite possibly different from that recommended for another cat presenting the same symptoms.

For many pet owners, one of the attractions of homeopathic treatment is the lack of side-effects — although these are also unusual with conventional therapies. A number of veterinary practices are now offering a combination of treatment methods, with homeopathy being one of the options.

Grooming &

Care

The amount of grooming care required will depend very much on your choice of cat. If you should pick the virtually hairless sphynx, grooming will not occupy any time at all, although you will need to keep your cat's skin clean and make sure that it is adequately protected from the sun if it goes outdoors on a hot day. By contrast, a Persian longhair, for example, will require careful daily grooming. Greater emphasis on grooming is particularly important when the cat is molting, to remove hair shed from the coat before it can be swallowed and create a furball in the stomach. Even wild cats such as lions can suffer from this problem. Bathing a cat may not be as problematical as you might expect, for, contrary to popular belief, many cats will tolerate or even enjoy being in water. Some, such as tigers and the Turkish Van, a domestic breed, frequently swim, while others, such as jaguars and the fishing cat, will hunt in the shallows.

HANDLING

Kittens can be handled without difficulty, and will not usually attempt to scratch or bite provided that their hindquarters are firmly supported.

Cats do not always appreciate being picked up, particularly if they are not used to being handled, so familiarize your kitten with this process from an early age.

Restraining and carrying

If a cat is frightened it will prove very difficult to restrain and handle, particularly if it is frightened. They will hiss and spit like their wild relatives, twisting their bodies adeptly, to make maximum use of their sharp claws and teeth. The cat will continue to behave in this way until it is free.

Such behavior is often displayed after traveling, particularly if the cat is not used to this experience. It may therefore be better, if time permits, to allow the cat to calm down, rather than attempting to lift it straight out of its carrying box. Carriers that have opening lids are better than those with

There are a number of ways of restraining a cat, to avoid being bitten. This method is useful for a close inspection of the head or eyes.

Cats can often become upset by a journey, and one way to lift a distressed cat into or out of a cat basket, is holding the scruff of the neck.

This way suits a fairly docile cat. Support is given to the hindquarters, to prevent the cat struggling from fear of being dropped.

doors at the front, simply because there is less possibility of the cat being able to hide away in the corner out of easy reach.

Picking up a cat

Under normal circumstances, however, it is not difficult to pick up a cat, particularly if it becomes used to this experience during kittenhood. If you have children, it is sensible to show them how to pick up the cat safely; otherwise there is a chance that either they or the cat could be hurt.

Start by putting your right hand under the cat's body between its front and hind legs, lifting it off the ground. Then place your left hand under its hindquarters to provide support. (If you are left-handed, simply reverse these positions.) Once the cat is settled in this position, make a fuss over it, so that it comes to feel comfortable being held.

Never allow the hindquarters to hang down unsupported, because this will be uncomfortable for the cat, and it will probably cling to you with its claws as it tries to prevent itself from falling to the floor. Similarly, do not hold the cat up in front of your face; it might feel insecure and catch your face with its claws.

Sometimes you may be faced with an uncooperative cat — perhaps when trying to give it a tablet. It wriggles around and resents being held, lashing out at you with its front paws when you try to open its mouth. In this case, a thick blanket or towel is likely to be helpful. Wrap the towel around the cat so that the edges cross in the back, keeping its troublesome forelegs wrapped inside, with just its head and neck protruding. Although this will not make your pet more friendly, it should mean that you can give the tablet relatively easily, with less fear of being injured, particularly if you use a pill gun.

If you do have the misfortune to be bitten or scratched in the process, always wash the wound as soon as possible, and seek medical advice if necessary. Otherwise, especially following a bite, you may find a painful and unpleasant septic wound may develop.

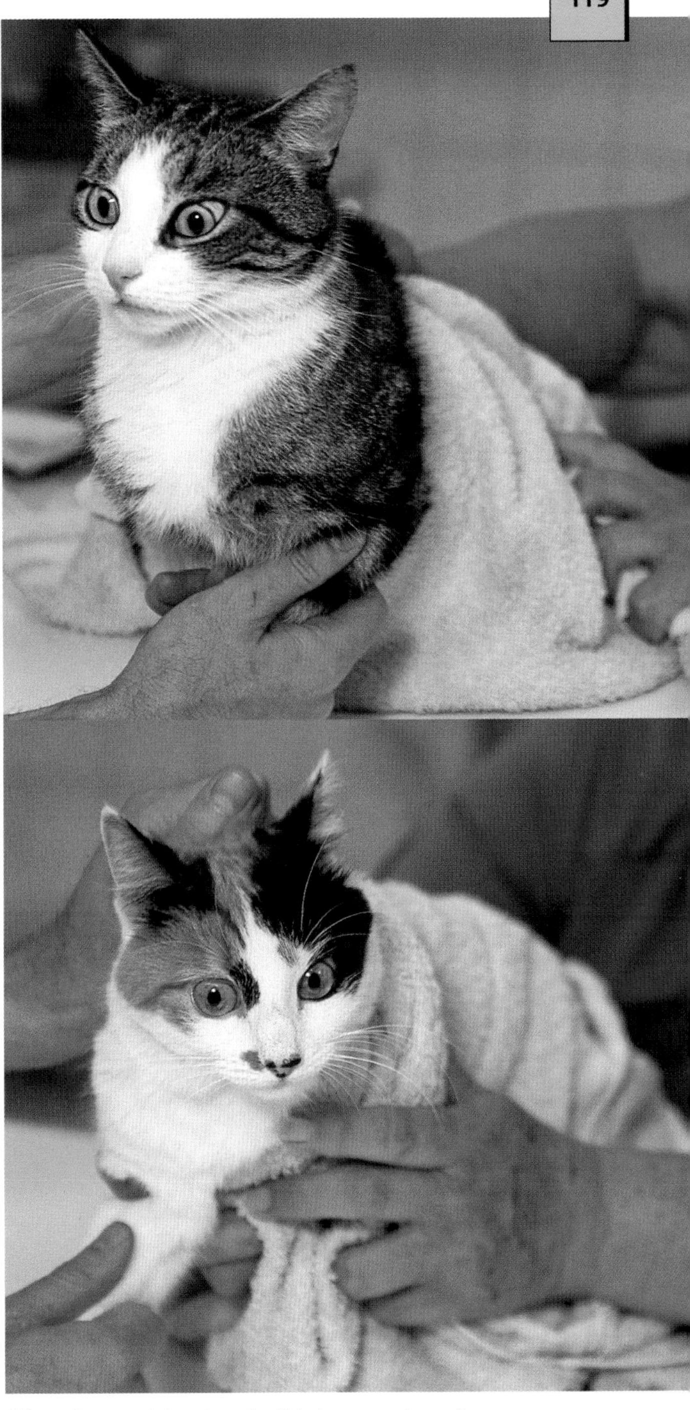

Wrapping a cat in a towel will help prevent you from being scratched. This method of handling is especially useful if you need to give your pet a pill which it is reluctant to take without a struggle. But remember you can still be bitten! It will help if someone else can hold the cat, and be sure to keep the towel pressed against the cat's body as it will still try to wriggle free.

GROOMING BASICS

A complicated grooming routine is not really necessary, even if you have a long haired cat. Tools to simplify this purpose are readily available from pet supply stores, and provided that the cat is used to being groomed from an early age, it is unlikely to resent this attention.

Be prepared for lengthy daily grooming sessions if you choose a long-haired cat. The coat will be thicker during the winter.

Grooming equipment

The basic equipment you will need are a brush and comb. For a long-haired cat, you may want to choose a combination comb, which has two sets of teeth on it, top and bottom. Start by using the broader set to remove any knots, and then refine the grooming process with the finer teeth. Where there are tangles, use a special detangling comb, the teeth of which will swivel, allowing the hairs to glide through the comb, rather than pulling at them.

A brush with natural bristles is generally preferable to one with synthetic bristles, as this is less likely to create static in the coat, which would cause the hairs to stand on end rather than lie flat.

For short-haired cats, a rubber brush is useful; this improves the blood circulation in the skin and acts as a general toner. A special grooming mitt, with a rubber palm consisting of short spikes, does a good job of removing excess fur and gives the cat a massage at the same time. Many cats love the sensation. If you are intending to exhibit your cat, you may also want a piece of clean chamois leather. You can use this to polish the cat's coat, giving it a striking gloss at the end of the grooming process. The other essential piece of grooming equipment will be a flea comb, which has especially fine teeth. Careful grooming serves to detect these parasites at an early stage.

Below *A wide range of grooming tools is now available to help keep your cat's coat in top condition.*

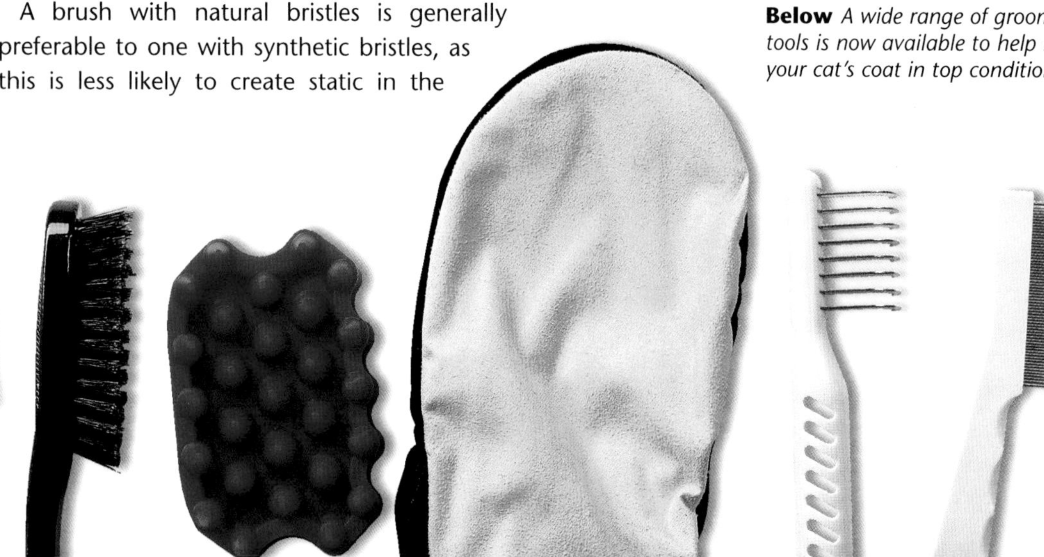

Different coat types

There are significant differences in the coat types of wild cats. Tigers from northern areas, such as Siberia, have longer and denser coats than those found in India and other more southerly parts of their range, close to the Equator. The same distinctions can be drawn in the case of wildcats. Not surprisingly, therefore, variations in the coats of domestic cats are well recognized and can be used for dividing them into groups.

Longhairs

It has often been suggested that the long-haired characteristic, found in Persians, for example, was first introduced by a cross-breeding involving Pallas's cat, but there appears to be no real evidence to support this view. Coat length is not a consistent feature in any event, as it may vary through the year.

Blue smoke Persian longhair.

Long-haired cats living in temperate areas look their most impressive during the winter, with their coats being at their most profuse at this time. In spring they will start to molt. The splendid ruff of the Maine coon, for example, will thin out and become far less prominent.

Red tabby American shorthair.

Shorthairs

Short-haired cats look sleeker than their long-haired relatives, and this is not just because of the length of the hairs themselves. Beneath the outer guard hairs of all cats, whether long-haired or short-haired, there is a softer bulky down, which helps to trap a layer of air close to the body. This air is warmed by the body's heat, and so has an insulating effect.

But, breeds of short-haired cat that originated in warmer climes have correspondingly less down, which means that their outer guard hairs have a sleeker appearance. It is also for this reason that tabby markings appear more vibrant in short-coated cats, simply because the dark hairs are lying closer to each other.

Variations

There are differences between the individual breeds, however, with the down and guard hairs of Persians being of almost equal length, while in the case of the Angora breed — thought to be the original long-haired cat and a native of warmer climes — the down hairs are relatively short.

The hair structure is very different in the case of the rex breeds. The Cornish rex has no guard hairs, and its coat is composed simply of down and the similarly short awn hairs, both of which have a natural tendency to curl. They have rather fragile hair that is easily damaged. The whiskers are also curled and typically are shorter than other cats.

The effect in the case of the pixie-like Devon rex is even more pronounced, although all three types of hair are present. Here the coat tends to be even thinner, with all the hairs resembling down. Wire-haired cats have hairs that are decidedly curled, somewhat like the wool on a sheep, while in the case of the sphynx, only traces of down hairs still remain on the body.

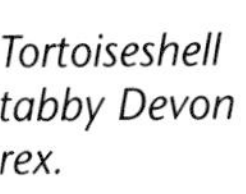

Tortoiseshell tabby Devon rex.

SELF-GROOMING

All cats spend considerable periods each day grooming themselves, and they may also groom other cats they know well, concentrating on the head and other areas of the body which would otherwise be out of reach. In hot weather, grooming may help the cat to cool down. It also gives a greater opportunity for the sunlight to reach the skin, triggering the synthesis of vitamin D here. This is vital for a healthy skeletal system, playing a key role in the calcium and phosphorus balance in the body.

Cats are fastidious groomers, spending long periods each day licking and caring for their coat. If your cat starts to become agitated when grooming, nibbling intently on one spot, this can be a sign of fleas. Some individuals become sensitized to flea saliva, resulting in an allergic reaction which requires veterinary treatment.

How Cats Care for their Coats

Domestic and wild female cats with young kittens will lick their offspring regularly from birth. In addition to cleaning their bodies, the mother cat's tongue, with its massaging effect, encourages the kittens to relieve themselves. A cat's grooming action also serves to pull dead hairs from the coat. This is achieved by the raised papillae on the cat's tongue, which give the tongue its characteristically rough texture.

Fur balls

Although it may not matter if a few hairs are swallowed, there will be a risk to the cat's health if large numbers are ingested, because these may form a solid mass in the stomach. The resulting fur ball is likely to cause an obstruction here, which will be reflected by a change in the cat's eating pattern. This is most likely in long-

Practical pointer

Older cats seem much more susceptible to fur balls than young ones. This may simply reflect the more sluggish activity within their older digestive tract. By grooming the cat regularly, you should be able to prevent this problem.

haired individuals when they are molting, and so shedding correspondingly more hair.

The cat will become more fussier than usual about its food, often displaying little appetite for the food when it is offered, and yet appearing to be constantly hungry. It will eat a little from its bowl as soon as the food is placed on the floor, and then ignore the rest. It will then return to eat further small portions later in the day, whereas in the past it would have cleared its bowl almost immediately.

There can be other possible causes of this behavior, most notably painful gums or teeth, and so it is advisable to take your cat to visit the veterinarian to establish the reason. If it is only a fur ball, a suitable laxative will usually lead to the passage of the fur ball out of the body. Cats may vomit up fur balls, rather than passing them out via the intestinal tract.

If a fur ball remains in a cat's stomach, it may become impregnated with mineral salts, taking on a stone-like appearance. This is sometimes seen in the case of lions, which may spit out one of these petrified fur balls before dying. In some areas it is believed that these stones have magical properties and if worn as a pendant protects the wearer from dangerous animals.

Practical Pointer

If the fur ball cannot be passed readily and continues to cause an obstruction, the only option may be for your veterinarian to remove it surgically.

BASIC INSTINCTS • Grooming activity

Wild cats will spend considerable periods of time grooming their fur each day when they are resting, using their rough tongues, covered with papillae, to remove dead hairs from the coat. Grooming also serves to keep the coat clean, removing any traces of blood from a previous kill which might attract flies; it can also help to cool the body. A female cat will groom her offspring. Mutual grooming of this type between older individuals is always suggestive of a strong bond between them.

Below *Cats are methodical about grooming. They can reach much of their body. But, mutual grooming (above) also strengthens bonds between individuals.*

Here the cat is licking the fur on its back. Saliva here will soon dry.

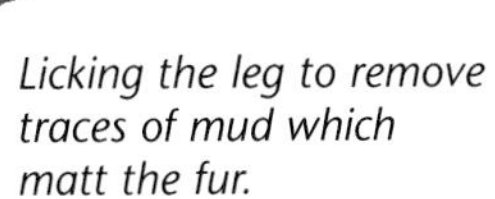

Licking the leg to remove traces of mud which matt the fur.

Paw licking not only cleans the paws, but will help to clean the face.

Often a cat will finish off its grooming session by licking down its sides.

WASHING

It is generally believed that cats dislike water, but in fact many wild cats, even tigers, are powerful swimmers and will enter water readily. Some will even catch food here — examples being the fishing cat of southeast Asia and the jaguar, which preys not only on fish but also on large aquatic reptiles.

The water myth

The domestic cat will also tolerate and even enjoy water. Cats will readily go outside in the rain and will play with a dripping faucet by pawing at the water as it falls. Again, it is partly a matter of conditioning, since cats that become used to water at an early stage in life are far less fearful of being bathed, for example, than those that have never had this experience.

It is not often necessary to bathe a cat, although for show purposes this may be required — particularly with white-haired cats — to ensure that they look their very best. In the case of a bad outbreak of fleas or other external parasites, such as lice, a medicated bath may be the most effective means of dealing with the infestation.

In terms of routine coat care, you can generally manage without having to wash the

Practical Pointer

Some cats have dirty ears, which may be cleaned carefully with a moist cotton swab, but do not probe into the ear canal itself. If your cat is scratching its ears frequently and you suspect that it may have an ear infection, consult your veterinarian.

Opposite *Tigers are one of the wild cats which will enter water without hesitation, and can swim effectively as well.*

cat entirely. Damp absorbent cotton (terry cloth) can be used to sponge areas of the coat that have become dirty, such as the fur around the mouth. In the case of a cat that has suffered from diarrhea and has stained fur around its rear, it will be preferable to trim off the contaminated area, rather than trying to wash it. A pair of blunt-ended scissors must be used.

Practical Pointer

If your cat's feet become covered with tar, possibly as the result of walking on a roof on a hot day, you must trim the fur and wash off any remaining deposits using a mild detergent. Do not allow your pet to lick the affected area, because it will ingest the tar. If it shows signs of discomfort in the mouth, it may already have done so; seek advice from your veterinarian.

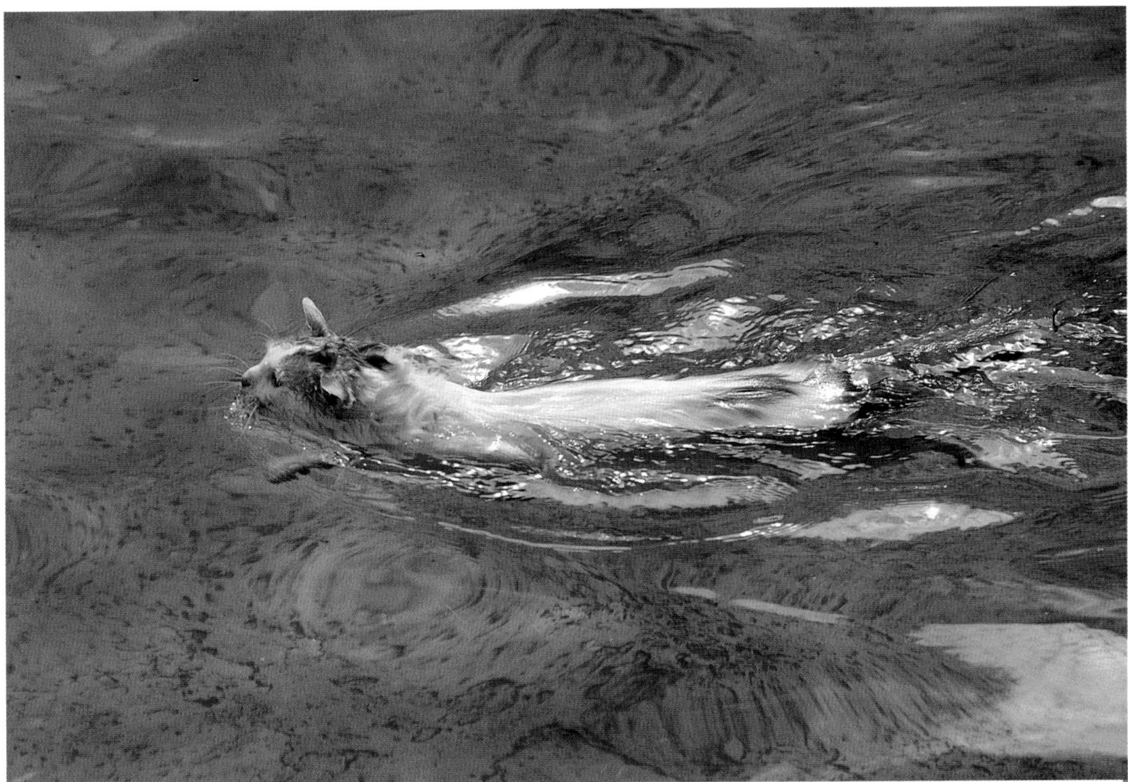

It is important to clean this area rapidly in any event, especially when the weather is warm because flies will be attracted here to lay their eggs. These will hatch rapidly into maggots, which bore into the cat's skin, releasing potentially deadly toxins into its body. If your cat has this problem seek veterinary help to clean the wound thoroughly, and give appropriate treatment.

BASIC INSTINCTS • Swimming cats

One breed of domestic cat — the Turkish Van (above) — displays a particularly close affiliation with water. It originates from the vicinity of Lake Van, in Turkey, where these cats will readily swim in the fresh water. The temperature in this part of the world can become very hot in the summer, and it could be that the cats have developed this unusual behavior as a means of cooling down.

Bathing a cat

Cats may not like the experience of being bathed at first, but in time, they can become accustomed to the experience. If possible, choose a fine day for bathing your cat, and do so outside. It is not very hygienic to use your own bathtub, and there is a risk that your pet might scratch it with its claws, should it become frightened. A baby bath is useful; otherwise a large plastic basin will do.

Before actually starting, have everything ready, so as not to upset the cat more than necessary beforehand. Partially fill the basin with tepid water. It will be helpful to have someone to hold the cat for you, while you concentrate on washing it. Wear gloves, particularly if you are giving the cat a medicated bath, and try to guard as much as possible against being bitten or scratched.

Start by lowering the cat cautiously into the water, allowing its back feet to make contact with the base of the bath, and then immerse its front feet also. If the cat is able to touch a solid surface, it will be less likely to struggle. A piece of rubber matting in the bottom may give it

Practical Pointer

When bathing your cat in the yard (or garden) it may be possible to attach a showerhead and a hose to a kitchen faucet and feed this out through a back door.

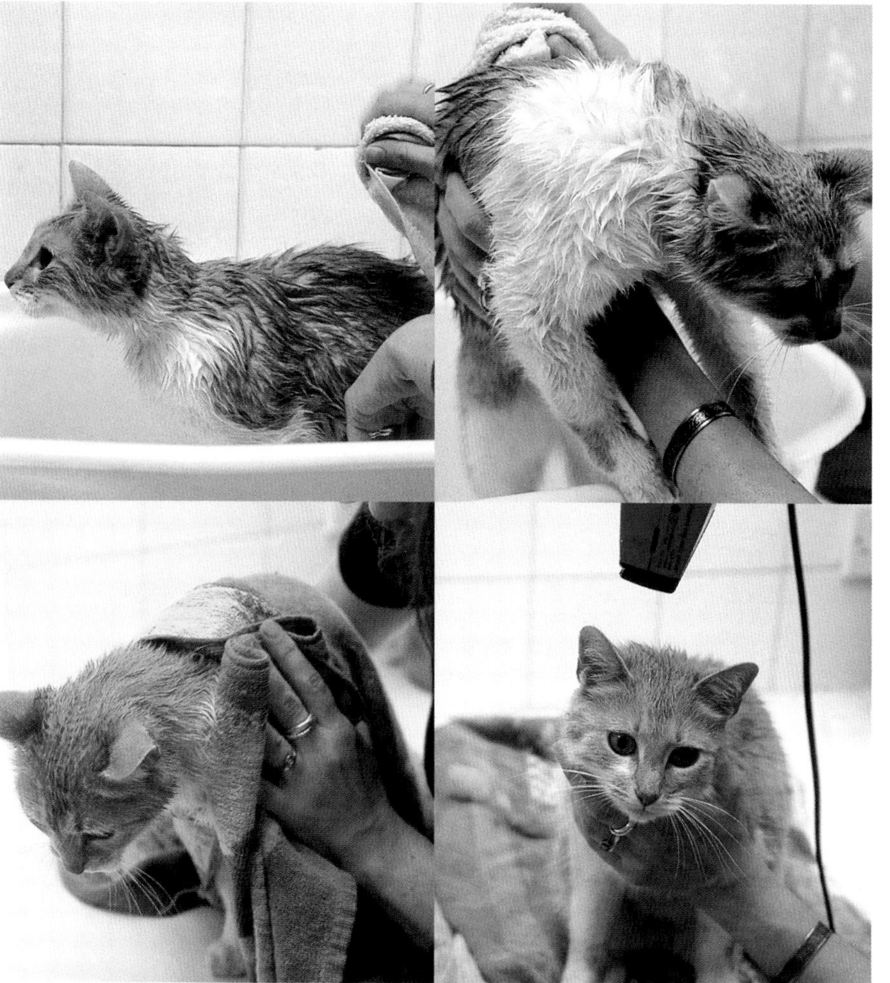

(Top left and right) *Choose a relatively shallow container, and partially fill it with tepid water before you place the cat in the bath. It may struggle a lot at this stage, so take particular care not to be scratched or bitten.*

(Bottom left) *Wet the cat's head last, taking care to avoid any shampoo entering the eyes. Rinse the coat and then wrap the cat in an old towel, before lifting it out of the bath.*

(Bottom right) *It may be possible to use a hair dryer on a cool setting to dry the coat, or alternatively, you can let the fur dry naturally.*

confidence. The water itself should not be too deep, a depth of about 4in (10cm) is adequate. The cat is less likely to panic if the water does not extend up the sides of its body.

You can then wet the coat, working from the hindquarters forwards, while taking particular care around the head. A small plastic measuring cup may be helpful for this purpose. To clean the coat itself, you can use either a special cat shampoo or a mild baby shampoo, but make sure in either case that it does not enter the cat's eyes.

Having worked the shampoo into the coat, rinse it off thoroughly, and wrap the cat in a towel, to remove excess water from the coat. Keep your pet warm while its coat dries. You may be able to use a hair dryer to speed up this process, although some cats will be alarmed by the resulting draft and the noise.

A bran bath

It is not always necessary to wash the cat in order to clean its coat. You can give a bran bath instead, which will remove excess grease. Heat the bran (which is sold in pet supply stores) on a tray in the oven until it is hot, and then while it is still warm rub this thoroughly into the cat's coat. After a few moments, the bran should have absorbed unwanted grease and can be brushed out. Most cats will tolerate a bran bath more readily than being soaked, but beware because it can be a very messy process, even with sheets of newspaper on the grooming table and around the floor to catch the flakes of bran.

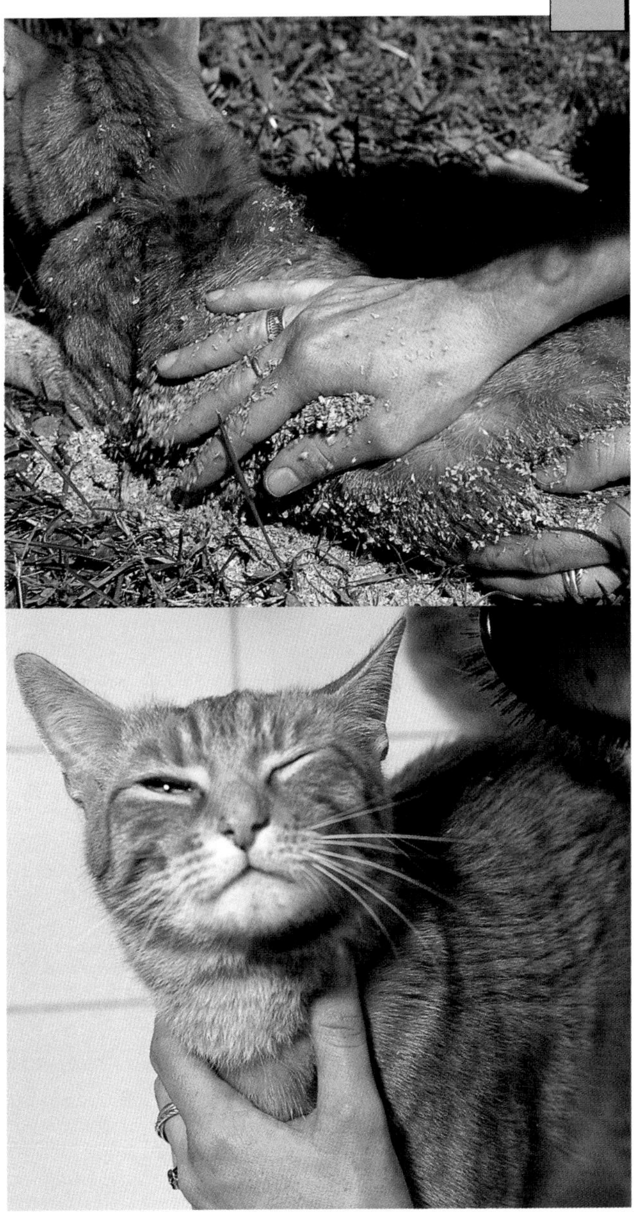

Above *A bran bath can be used to remove excess oil from the coat, without having to wet the cat. It is often used by exhibitors before cat shows. The bran is warmed in the oven and then rubbed thoroughly into the coat before being brushed out again. This is a messy procedure, so carry it out either outdoors, or in a part of the home where it will be easy to clean up the bran afterward.*

Practical Pointer

Check the temperature setting on your hair dryer before using it. It should not be too hot, because this will prove very uncomfortable for your cat, and might even burn its skin.

CAT COATS AND MARKINGS

Above *The striking appearance of many wild cats such as the jaguar has seen them being hunted almost to extinction in some cases for their pelts.*

Wild cats have been hunted for their fur for centuries. In fact, the earliest record of cat skins being worn dates back to 6500 B.C., and comes from Anatolia in Turkey. Archeological evidence from this area has revealed that leopard skins were used for clothing. They may also have had a symbolic significance. It seems to have been a fairly widespread early belief that garments made from the skins of these powerful mammals conveyed strength to the wearer.

Fur trade to cat fancy

More recently, a number of wild cat species, including jaguar and cheetah, have been heavily hunted for their pelts. This is partly because of the texture of the fur but also because of its very attractive appearance. The trade in wild cats' skins is now very tightly controlled, and in some cases even banned, to conserve the remaining

The markings of a mackerel tabby, so-called because the lines are said to resemble fish bones.

In the spotted form of the tabby, dark lines are broken up to form spots, separated by lighter areas of fur.

Practical Pointer

Details of forthcoming shows that you might want to visit are usually to be found in the pages of many of the cat magazines which are now available, either by subscription or from newsstands.

populations. Clothing manufacturers are resorting to fake fur by way of replacement.

The patterning of wild cats may look superficially similar, but in reality the markings are all different, so that a careful observer can recognize individuals without difficulty. It may be the pattern of spotting in the case of the leopard cat, or the stripes on the head of tigers, but each is unique. The markings are present in kittenhood and remain consistent throughout their lives.

The same applies in the case of those domestic breeds that have a spotted patterning, although in these cases, there tends to be a stronger tendency toward uniformity in the case of purebred stock, owing to the judging standards that have been laid down for show purposes.

The cat fancy

The origins of these standards date back to the start of the cat fancy, when judges required a means of distinguishing winners from the rest. The standard lays down what is considered to be the ideal, in terms of the variety concerned, and the cats are each judged against the standard, rather than against other cats in their class.

The cat fancy developed in Victorian Britain — the word "fancy" being a general term that was used in this period to describe the selective breeding of livestock and plants for exhibition purposes. Similar organizations have been founded in other countries. Today's purebred cats differ significantly in appearance from those seen in the 1800s, however, and this has been reflected in changes to the standards over the years.

BASIC INSTINCTS • Coat variations

The black markings of the serval shown here, can be highly variable. Those from grassland areas have larger spots than those living in forest regions. The basic coat coloration of all wildcats is fairly similar, often being a sandy shade, with the coat marked with black blotches or stripes. There is none of the range of colors or markings associated with today's domestic breeds. Regional variations do occur, with lighter-colored individuals being seen in more open country. Siberian tigers are another example of a local shift; their pale coats help them to blend in against the snow which may occur in their area for several months of the year. Camouflage is important for predators, so they can approach their prey undetected.

Natural variants

The emergence of the wide range of colors now seen in the domestic cat owes much to selective breeding over the course of the past century or so. However, color variants also occur among wild populations of cats. In some cases, they are quite widely distributed.

Nevertheless, the likelihood of a color variant actually surviving in the wild is relatively remote. This is because mutations of this type are genetically recessive, which means that if an abnormally colored cat mates with a typical example of the species, none of the resulting offspring will show the unusual coloration.

Only half of the offspring, on average, will even carry the mutant gene, and they in turn would need to mate with another individual possessing the same mutant gene to have any hope of producing offspring of their own that display it. Mutant genes therefore soon become swamped in a wild population.

Humans can best ensure the survival of such mutations, and even enable their numbers to rise rapidly. Under controlled conditions specific pairings can be made to maximize the number of abnormally colored offspring.

Melanistic cats that are characterized by predominantly black fur, are more common among wild species than leucistic cats — those lacking any black pigment — although among tigers this trait is rare: There is only one verified record of a melanistic tiger.

Black panthers, which are actually the melanistic form of the leopard, are not unusual. The tendency toward melanism is most marked in cats that live in forested areas, where presumably, the change in coat color conceals their presence more effectively. The underlying patterning can still be seen at close quarters, however, and these melanistic individuals will live alongside and breed with normally colored cats.

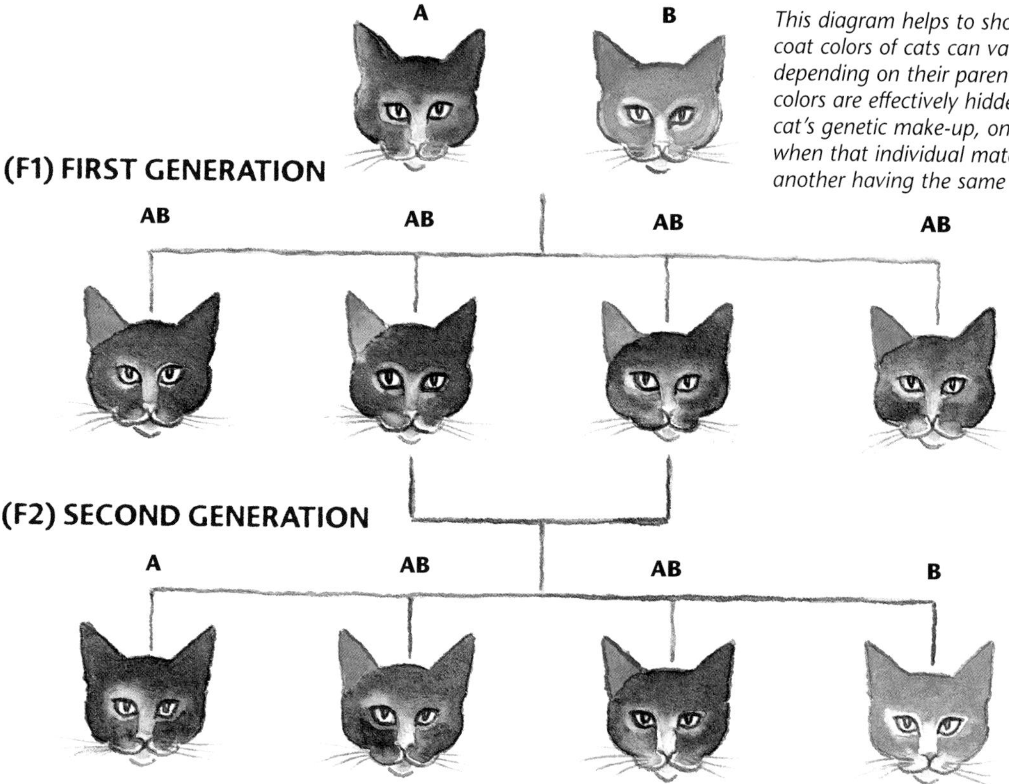

This diagram helps to show how the coat colors of cats can vary, depending on their parentage. Some colors are effectively hidden in the cat's genetic make-up, only emerging when that individual mates with another having the same gene.

Practical Pointer

Appearances can be deceptive: There are two distinctive forms of the jaguarundi — gray and red. Early zoologists classified them as two different species, calling the red variant the eyra, until it was realized they were the same species.

BASIC INSTINCTS • White tigers

Among the wild cats, the so-called "white" tiger is the best example of a color change. These tigers are markedly paler than the ordinary Bengal tigers found in northern, eastern and central parts of India where they occur. Their distribution is concentrated in Rewa state, where they were first reported more than 160 years ago. A breeding program to safeguard the future of these unusually colored tigers was begun during the 1950s by the Maharaja of Rewa, and today stock is widely distributed in zoos throughout the world.

CARE OF CATS

Cats tend to suffer more from gum disease than actual tooth decay, but erosion of the gum margin can lead to the loss of teeth.

Domestic cats are relatively easy pets to look after, because they generally have a robust constitution. Neverthless, regular veterinary check-ups, particularly as the cat gets older, can be beneficial as preventing the build-up of tartar on its teeth will help the cat's general health.

Teeth

The mouths of wild cats are equipped with a formidable array of teeth, as is the mouth of the domestic cat. But on occasion something goes wrong during a hunt, and then one or more of the pointed canine teeth can be broken. This can happen if the cat bites into solid bone, for example, and the tooth is already weakened.

Such an accident is potentially serious for a wild cat, which needs a full, or nearly full complement of teeth in order to survive. By contrast, a domestic cat can lose quite a few teeth as it approaches old age, with no ill effect. There is now growing awareness, however, that if you take care of your cat's teeth from the early days, there is a greater prospect of their remaining healthy throughout the cat's life.

Although it may not inconvenience an older cat greatly if it has lost a few of its teeth, this may make it difficult for the cat to eat tough or dry foods, for example. It would then need to be fed on canned food, which it could consume much more easily.

Gingivitis

Cats do not suffer from dental decay in the same way as people do. It is, rather, a build-up of tartar on the gum margins that is the problem. This extends to the base of the teeth, leading to erosion of the gums and ultimately weakening the teeth in their sockets. Signs of gingivitis — inflammation of the gums — will be noted; that is, the gums will appear reddish rather than pink.

Prevention of gingivitis, which is a common symptom of periodontal disease, is easily accomplished by having tartar removed regularly before it can cause harm. The cat's diet may also be significant; those fed on dried food are far less susceptible to accumulations of tartar, because they chew their food more thoroughly before swallowing it. As a consequence, more of the tooth is used, and the tartar is wiped off.

Your cat may allow you to brush its teeth, particularly if you train it to do so from kittenhood. Special kits comprising a toothbrush and special toothpaste can be used,

Practical Pointer

You may want to provide your cat with a toy it can chew, to help prevent the build-up of tartar.

Practical Pointer

Do not use ordinary toothpaste to clean your cat's teeth; cats dislike its taste, and this can make it difficult to brush their teeth again in the future.

although sodium bicarbonate (baking soda) powder is also suitable for this purpose.

Get someone else to hold the cat for you, and brush the teeth carefully, to avoid causing bleeding. This task should ideally be carried out once a week. Aside from preventing accumulations of tartar, it should also help to freshen your cat's breath.

Older cats with bad teeth may be reluctant to eat properly, contorting their mouths so that they can avoid using a painful tooth. They may also drop food out of their mouths and drool saliva. Although by this stage it will be too late to prevent the dental decay, it is possible to relieve the pain by removing the affected teeth and treating the gingivitis.

BASIC INSTINCTS • Vital canines

While domestic cats can manage without their teeth, eating canned food for example, missing canines especially can spell disaster for cats in the wild, because they depend on those teeth to kill their prey. This jaguar has broken the tips of its canines — these will not regrow.

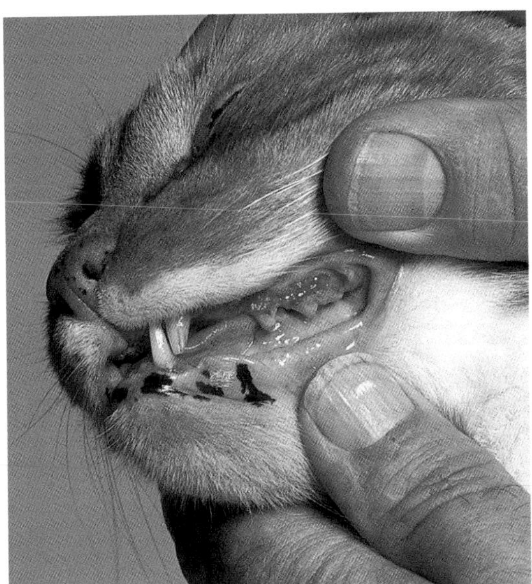

Above *Note the reddish inflammation of the gum, which would normally be pink, and the accumulation of dirty brown tartar on the teeth themselves.*

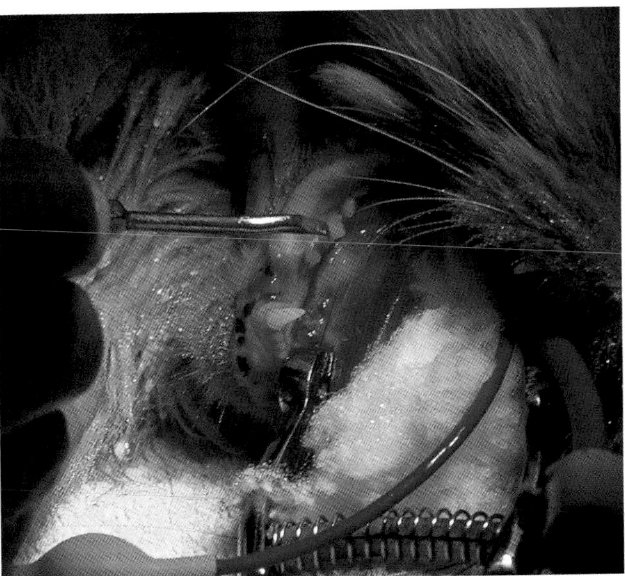

Above *This cat has been anesthetized so that its teeth can be properly cleaned. Bad teeth are one of the main causes of halitosis (bad breath) in cats.*

Left *The claws are important to allow wild cats to catch hold of their quarry, as well as defend themselves in fights. Scratching at tree bark in this way helps to ensure that the tips of the claws remain really sharp.*

Claws

Cats depend on their claws to help them climb, as well as to seize and restrain their prey. They will also use their claws to mark their territory and when fighting, lashing out and inflicting painful swipes with their feet.

On occasion a cat's claws may need trimming — particularly in the case of older cats, which are less likely to wear them down. It is the so-called dew claw, on the inside of each of the front legs, corresponding to the human thumb, that is most likely to become a problem. As its name suggests, it is not in contact with the ground, but skims over the surface of the grass becoming soaked with dew.

There is a real risk that this claw will grow around and curl back on itself, to the extent of penetrating the pad, which will be very painful for the cat. This overgrowth occurs because, in domestic cats especially, this claw is unlikely to be subjected to any wear unless the cat is a habitual hunter.

On occasion, you may find a piece of claw on the floor in the house. This is not a sign of injury, but rather an indication that the cat has chewed at its nail, removing the outer cuticle. If you inspect the paws closely, you will see that the nails are all still present, although some may be shorter than others.

Practical Pointer

If the claw does start to bleed, place a folded piece of damp absorbent cotton (cotton wool) on the tip, and hold it firmly in place to encourage clotting. Blood loss under these circumstances should only be minimal.

Clipping claws

In cases where the cat is not scratching regularly and wearing down its claws, it is important to trim them back, before they become a cause of inconvenience or pain — to the cat or to others. This can be accomplished quite easily with a suitable pair of clippers (see opposite top right), but you may prefer to take your cat to the veterinarian for this purpose.

Should you decide to go ahead on your own, obtain a robust pair of clippers designed for this purpose. Do not rely on scissors, as they will simply split the claw. To reveal the claws, press gently on the pad of the foot. It is very important to ensure that you have good light, so that you can then easily locate the blood supply to each claw. This will be visible as a thin pinkish streak running a short way down each claw toward the tip.

The correct place to cut is a short distance below the end of this line, to avoid causing the nail to bleed. Have someone else restrain the cat firmly for you, so that you can hold the cat's foot securely, knowing that it will not move as you cut the nail, since this might have serious consequences. If the clipped claw appears slightly flaky around the edge, file the area gently with a nail file.

Right *Special nail clippers not scissors should be used, to ensure the nail is cut cleanly, and not splintered.*

Above *Cats generally do not resent having their claws trimmed, but a nervous cat can be wrapped in a blanket to reduce the risk of you being scratched. Do the cutting in a good light to ensure that you do not clip the nail too short.*

Practical Pointer

Cutting the claws simply to stop your cat from scratching furniture will not work. It may even encourage this behavior, since the cat will then seek to sharpen them on an attractive surface.

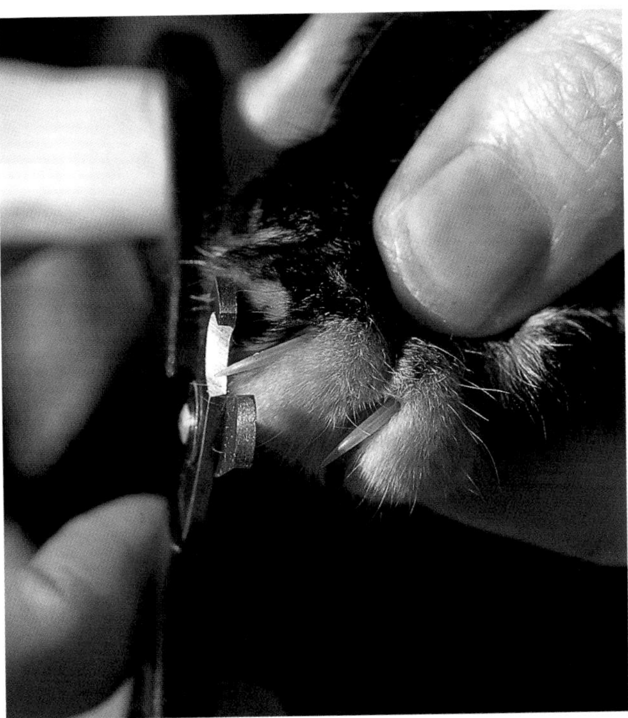

Above *When clipping the claws, it is vital to support the cat's foot, so that you can cut the claw properly. This is similar to trimming your own nails — it should not be painful for your pet, provided that you do not cut the claws too short.*

Eyes

A cat's eyes will rarely need attention, although cats can sometimes injure them when walking through undergrowth. One eye will then appear swollen and partially or even totally shut, while the other is completely unaffected. In other cases, where the nictitating membrane is visible, then this is likely to be more indicative of a generalized illness, and loss of condition rather than any direct trauma.

Bathing the eyes may be necessary to remove traces of tear staining here. Never be tempted to use a cotton swab for this task, because there is a risk that it could stab the cat in the eye if your pet moves forward unexpectedly.

Above *Examining a kitten's eye. Scratches on the surface of the eye can occur, and are likely to need veterinary treatment. One of the earliest signs that something is wrong may be repeated blinking.*

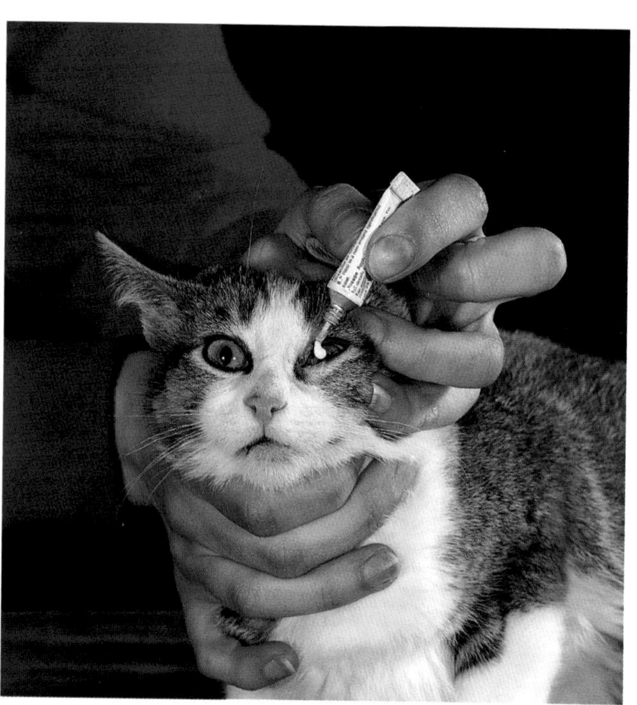

Above *Applying antibiotic ointment to the eye. Restrain the cat carefully as shown, taking care to ensure that the ointment is directed away from the eye rather than toward it. Several applications a day are likely to be necessary.*

Again, it will be helpful to have someone holding the cat while you concentrate on attending to its eye. In this case, with a relatively friendly cat, ask your companion to restrain the cat with its back turned toward their body, on a table at a convenient height.

The helper's hands should then extend around the sides of the cat's body, holding it reasonably tightly and meeting on the upper part of the cat's chest, just below the neck. In

Practical Pointer

Do not be tempted to keep an ophthalmic medicine after you have completed the recommended course of treatment. Any that is left over should be disposed of safely; once opened, these products have a relatively short shelf-life.

this position, the cat should be adequately restrained and unable to raise its front paws easily to scratch you or your helper, while you are bathing its eye. Wrapping the cat in a towel may also be helpful.

Eyedrops

Cats are generally fairly tolerant about having their eyes bathed, simply closing the eye, allowing you to wipe gently down the sides and over the lids. The same applies when you have to give eyedrops or apply an ointment, although an element of luck is required, especially with drops, to ensure that the cat does not blink before the medicine reaches the surface of the eye, as it is then likely to be wasted on the eyelids.

If this does happen, it is usually safest to repeat the dose. Regular treatment of eye ailments, several times a day as directed, is essential, because the tear fluids will wash the medication quite rapidly out of the eye, and it will need to be topped up to maintain a therapeutic level.

Ophthalmic ointment can be applied more easily than drops, simply because you can see it. With the cat adequately restrained, squeeze the medication across the junction of the eyelids. Once the cat opens its eyes, the ointment will then flow into the eye itself, although it is often a good idea to hold on to the cat for a few moments afterwards, to give the ointment an opportunity to dissolve. Otherwise the cat may simply wipe the ointment away with its paw.

Practical Pointer

If the ointment will not flow readily, warming the tube slightly under a running hot faucet may help. The flow of ointment should then be more even. Do not press too hard, otherwise it will spurt out.

If you need to clean the fur around your cat's eye, then gently wipe the area with damp cotton (cotton wool), in a direction away from the eye rather than toward it. Most cats will not struggle too much under these circumstances.

Ears

Cat's ears are often torn and injured in fights, but because they consist essentially of cartilage, they are reasonably robust and will not normally bleed significantly. If your cat comes home with a torn ear, you should bathe the ear and treat it with antiseptic ointment. It should heal uneventfully, although your cat will probably be scarred for life. Battling toms often show lines of torn places and bites along the sides of their ears.

The ears will sometimes need cleaning, but if you suspect that there could be an infection within the ear, you should take your cat to the veterinarian, who will be able to look down into this section of the ear with an otoscope and seek the source of the problem. Often ear infections are of mixed origin, resulting from the combined presence of fungi, bacteria, and minute ear mites.

Above *Scratching of the ear is often a sign of an infection within — check for signs of dirt by looking gently in the ear canal, and sniffing for any trace of an unpleasant odor.*

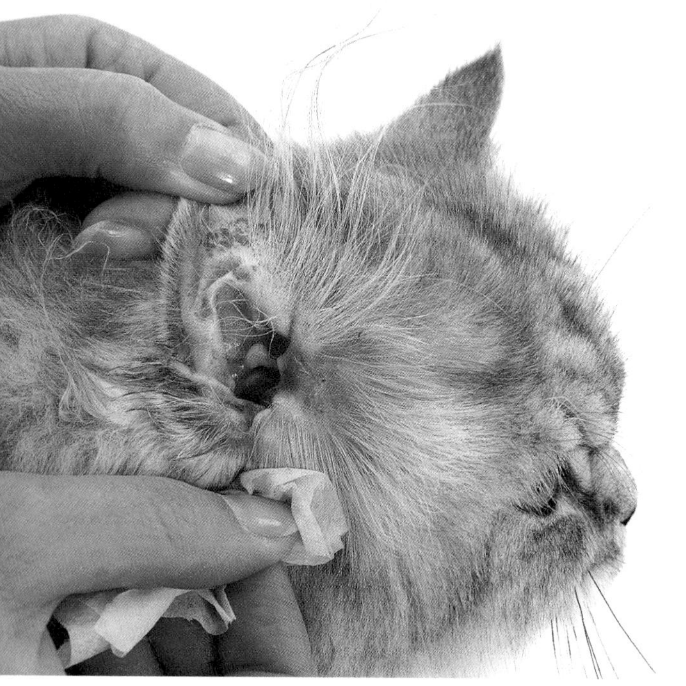

Above *Wipe the external part of the ear with damp cotton (cotton wool) to clean it, but avoid probing down inside the ear, because this can result in injury.*

The presence of mites, in particular, is likely to lead to the presence of dark matter in the visible part of the ear canal, and this can be removed carefully with absorbent cotton (cotton wool) and a little olive oil poured into the ear canal. Remember, however, that your cat may well be in pain and could resent having its ears treated in this fashion.

Ear drops

When giving ear drops, be sure to place the medication well down within the ear canal, rather than allowing the drops to fall on the

Practical pointer

Always seek prompt treatment for ear infections, because they can spread to the inner ear, affecting the cat's sense of balance.

Practical Pointer

If you use a cotton swab be careful not to push wax and debris farther down into the ear canal, causing a plug here.

cartilage. It can help to rub the area around the base of the ear, to ensure that the medicine is evenly distributed. Continue the course of treatment until the end, as always; ear infections can be very difficult to eliminate in some cases and may become chronic. The cat will appear to recover for a brief time, but then the infection develops again soon after the treatment stops.

An infection is not the only reason as to why a cat's ears may be painful, although other causes tend to be more seasonal. A grass seed may become lodged in the ear canal, for example, setting up a major irritation. Your veterinarian may even have to sedate your pet in order to examine it properly under these circumstances, removing the seed with a pair of fine forceps.

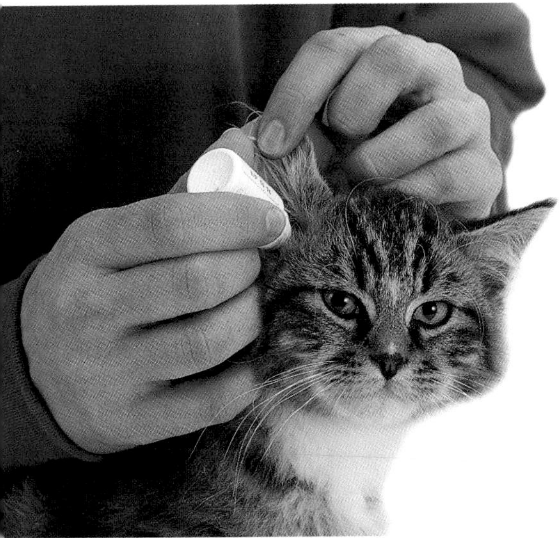

Above *When applying drops, place the nozzle in proximity to the ear canal, and afterward, gently massage the outer part of the ear to cause the medication to flow down here.*

BASIC INSTINCTS • Big ears

Injured and torn ears are not uncommon among male wild cats, for this part of the body can easily be damaged in a fight. Just like domestic cats, wild cats such as this cheetah may scratch the fur from their ears if they are bothered by parasites infecting them.

The ears are more prominent in the case of those wild cats, such as servals, that rely on them to detect their prey. The large earflaps serve to trap the ultrasonic calls of rodents, so that the cat is then able to pinpoint its prey easily, even when the animal is obscured by grass. The shape of the ears can also be affected by the wild cat's environment. In the case of the desert-dwelling sand cat, both its external ears and the auditory bullae within the ears are enlarged.

The bigger earflaps may help the cat to dissipate heat from its body and also locate the sound effectively, in the relative quiet of this landscape. The bullae help to isolate the sounds of potential prey easily, against a background where rodents can blend in and burrow out of sight with relative ease.

Dealing with mood changes

Cats are affected by a variety of experiences in their lives, and their behavior may change as a result. This conditioning explains why some populations of big cats such as lions and tigers develop into man-eaters. Once they have killed people, they continue to do so, because people are easy quarry. We have none of the alert senses of herbivores for example, nor keen night vision. We are unable to outrun these cats; and if caught, we lack the strength to fight them off.

In the case of man-eating lions, the only effective course of action is to wipe out the pride by shooting them. With tigers, however, a different approach has had some success. Since these cats dislike attacking from the front, giving special masks to people working in areas where man-eating tigers are present has proved beneficial; the masks are worn with the faces toward the back, fooling the tiger into thinking that the person — with his/her back to the tiger — is actually confronting it. This ploy has reduced the incidence of attacks on humans. It has been suggested that the shortage of fresh water in the parts of India where man-eating tigers occur may be responsible for this aggression.

Catnip

One of the most interesting changes in cat behavior can be induced by the plant known as catnip or catmint (*Nepeta cataria*). It appears to be a genetically mediated response, linked with a dominant gene, which means that most, but not all, cats in a population will respond to this plant. Nor is it just domestic cats that are affected by it — even tigers and snow leopards will respond in the same way.

They start by sniffing the plant, and then may nibble it; then they roll over and become very relaxed. It is unclear as to why catnip has this effect, but it may be due to the fact that its active ingredient, nepetalactone, is similar to marijuana. An alternative suggestion is that it is similar to the chemicals produced by the female in estrus, although in the case of catnip, both male and female cats will respond to it. Manufacturers often use various extracts of this herb in cat toys to enhance their appeal.

Practical pointer

Catnip can be easily cultivated from seed in a garden, for the delectation of your cat. It is a perennial and does not have strong soil preferences, though it does need to be kept moist. Keep it well protected until it is established; otherwise your cat may love it to death. Another possible hazard is that the catnip may attract the neighbors' cats to your garden.

This cat is rolling on a sprig of catnip — a herb which is grown in many gardens, and which holds a particular fascination for cats, both wild and domestic, although not all individuals will respond to it.

Above *Thanks to advances in nutritional and veterinary fields, domestic cats are now living longer than ever — usually well into their teens. This particular cat is seventeen years old, and is as playful as ever.*

Older cats

The life expectancy of domestic cats has risen dramatically, even over the course of the past decade, and it is not unusual for them to live well into their teens. This is much longer than many of the wild cats, which face a much more hazardous existence.

Part of the reason for this increasing longevity is that owners are now more aware of the fact that it is possible to delay the signs of aging, by taking the cat for regular veterinary check-ups. Although some illnesses are still resistant to treatment — chronic renal (kidney) failure is an example — careful dietary management may offset the worst effects for a year or more, extending the cat's life as a consequence. A careful watch on diet can also help counteract obesity and heart disease.

Regular veterinary checks every six months or so are recommended from the age of seven or eight years onward. Physically, cats show relatively few external signs of aging; black cats, for example, do not turn gray. It is not unusual for cats to lose some weight, though, with their body feeling bonier as a consequence.

Practical Pointer

Do not force your cat to sit on your lap as it becomes older, because this position may no longer be as comfortable for it.

Above *Wild cats have a much shorter life expectancy than their domestic relatives, rarely living for more than about ten years. A combination of factors, including malnutrition and a heavy parasitic burden in some cases, contributes to their early demise. In zoological collections, their life expectancy is generally much longer.*

Practical Pointer

Vitamin and mineral supplements may be useful for older cats. Your veterinarian will advise you.

INDEX

CREDITS

Quarto would like to acknowledge and thank the following for providing pictures used in this book. While every effort has been made to acknowledge copyright holders we would like to apologize should there have been any omissions.

Key: t=top b=below c=center
l=left r=right

David Alderton p.39, p.72, p.81b, p.106b, p.109; **Animal Photography** p.34, p.60, p.70, p.84b, p.132, p.141; **Marc Henrie** p.29, p.42, p.50, p.52, p.56, p.97b, p.101, p.112t, p.113t, p.114b, p.118, p.133bl; **Jacana** p.35, p.71, p.94, p.100t, p.102b, p.114t, p.134; **Pictor International** p.62, p.87b; **Tony Stone Images** p.91; **Bruce Tanner Photographer** p.1t, p.31, p.33, p.45, p.46, p.47t, p.51, p.63, p.65l, p.79, p.87t, p.97t, p.103, p.105b, p.108b, p.124, p.128, p.129, p.131, p.133t, p.141r; **Warren Photographic** p.1b, p.2, p.3, p.4l, p.4r, p.5, p.6, p.7, p.15, p.17, p.19, p.21t, p.23, p.24, p.25, p.26, p.28t, p.28b, p.30l&r, p.37t&b, p.43, p.47b, p.48, p.49, p.54, p.59, p.64, p.65r, p.66t, p.67, p.68, p.69, p.73, p.74, p.75, p.76, p.77, p.78, p.81t, p.84t, p.85, p.86, p.89, p.93r, p.95, p.96, p.98, p.102t, p.104, p.107r, p.108t, p.112b, p.116, p.117, p.122, p.123, p.125, p.136t&b, p.137, p.138t&b, p.139t&b, p.140; **Windrush Photos** p.14, p.111b.

Quarto would like to thank the following for supplying props and equipment for photography:
The Streatham Hill Veterinary Surgery
101 Sternhold Avenue
Streatham Hill
SW2

Petsmart House
Dorcan Complex
Faraday Road
Swindon
SN3 5HQ